ADVANCE PRAISE

"A terrific set of stories and guiding metaphors from a successful global business executive—this book is perfect for the business school student looking for great real-world examples of key concepts they learned in their leadership and organizational behavior classes."

—DOLLY CHUGH, ASSOCIATE PROFESSOR AT NEW YORK UNIVERSITY STERN SCHOOL OF BUSINESS

"With this book, Vishal Agarwal is the mentor everyone wishes they had in the corporate world. He demystifies the social dynamics of the global corporation through apt metaphors that quickly cut to the attitudes and behaviors essential to the success of the ambitious young manager. Read it, and learn how to hack your path in the corporate jungle without putting out an eye."

—KATE SWEETMAN, AUTHOR, LEADERSHIP AUTHORITY, AND FORMER EDITOR AT *HARVARD BUSINESS REVIEW*

"As an educator and corporate coach, I am blessed to meet some of the most accomplished business people and innovative corporate executives. Vishal Agarwal is one of the best. His new book is a gift to anyone reaching for the pinnacle of corporate success."

—PAUL SANDERS, OB, PROFESSOR AT INSEAD

"Give to Get shows that in this connected age, the best advice is a mix of both experience and intellect. Author Vishal Agarwal delivers both in this must-read!"

—DAVE KERPEN, CEO OF LIKEABLE AND *NEW YORK TIMES* BEST-SELLING AUTHOR OF *THE ART OF PEOPLE*

"As an international TV journalist who has spent my career focussing on the facts and figures, it's reassuring to see Vishal give an honest assessment of life in the corporate world. True leadership is a rare thing—and having a guide to seeking it and achieving it is invaluable. I particularly enjoyed the advice Vishal gives in his chapter "The Lion and the Goat," strongly encouraging the aspiring corporate executive to endure what is always a very tough path to success."

—RIZ KHAN, INTERNATIONAL BROADCASTER AND JOURNALIST

"From Africa to the world, Give to Get provides a global sense that no matter what side of the Atlantic we are on, we all need a book like this to guide us. It is a phenomenal inside lane to the top."

—HUBERT DANSO, CEO AND VICE CHAIRMAN OF AFRICA INVESTORS (AI) GROUP

GIVE TO GET

A SENIOR LEADER'S GUIDE TO
NAVIGATING CORPORATE LIFE

GIVE
TO
GET

VISHAL AGARWAL

LIONCREST
PUBLISHING

GIVE TO GET

A Senior Leader's Guide to Navigating Corporate Life

ISBN   978-1-61961-829-9 *Hardcover*

         978-1-61961-828-2 *Paperback*

         978-1-61961-827-5 *Ebook*

To the three most important women in my
life: my wife and my two daughters.

My ten-year-old who thinks she is sixteen,
my sixteen-year-old who is approaching twenty-one, and
my forty-five-year-old who wants to be twenty-five.

My life at home shapes my outlook on all the things I do—the drama,
the decibels, the color, the voice of reason, and the "You're not as
important as you think you are" that all happen at home daily.

To Bianca, Roshni, and Mira.
Life without you would be meaningless.

CONTENTS

INTRODUCTION..11

1. THE LION AND THE GOAT..........................17

2. A CULTURE-WITHIN-A-CULTURE...............31

3. MAPPING OUT YOUR STAKEHOLDERS.......61

4. ACTIONS ARE LOUDER THAN WORDS......85

5. TAKING YOUR CREDIT TO THE BANK 101

6. NO PLACE TO GO BUT UP..........................113

7. OVERCOMING UNDERWHELM 123

8. OVERCOMING BURNOUT 133

CONCLUSION..143

ABOUT THE AUTHOR 145

ABOUT THE AUTHOR ....

INTRODUCTION

YOUR JOURNEY TO THE
C-SUITE STARTS HERE

Over the last twenty-four years, I've been fortunate enough to experience all the perks and benefits of a high-powered corporate career. Jetting off to interesting locales, being called away for luxurious business travel, flying in private jets. Meeting business moguls, world leaders, and corporate celebrities. Working with high-ranking government officials in two dozen countries, eating like a king, and being wined and dined at grandiose corporate events. It's been epic, and I wouldn't change a thing.

But that's not what this book is about.

A corporate career can also feel like a never-ending grind. Endless meetings, frustrating bureaucracy, rigid fiefdoms and silos. Constant travel, overnight flights followed by 8:00 a.m. meetings, and late-night conference calls. High stress, rivers of coffee, and seemingly endless time away from family. Working for a large corporation can be a thrilling ride, but it's also full of aggressive competition, petty jealousy and skepticism, intense scrutiny from all angles, and myriad obstacles, challenges, and pitfalls.

If you know how to navigate these challenges, they'll become your strength and fuel your success. But if you don't, they can destroy your career and cost you everything you've worked so hard for. I've seen countless senior leaders who were very talented and hard-working, but didn't know how to navigate. In all cases, they ended up feeling unwanted and unrecognized, had their egos bruised and their reputations battered, and ultimately left the company.

The life of a senior corporate leader is arduous and demanding. For every deal-closing dinner and big win, there are dozens of battles with fierce competitors and brain damage with internal stakeholders. I've therefore come to believe that one of the essential skills in the corporate world is *endurance*. There is no dearth of smart, talented young executives, but many of them lack the ability, willingness, and fortitude to endure. Anyone who lacks the grit to stay in the marathon of corporate life will quickly find themselves on the outside.

ALL THE RIGHT REASONS

Most ambitious business school graduates enter corporate life with good intentions and boundless energy, passion, and excitement. They join big companies to develop their skills and build an impressive resume. They want to establish credibility and grow their reputation—to get a seat at the table. Along the way, many of them generate some stability and earn a consistent paycheck, then they get married and buy a home.

Then the trouble starts.

Many executives start to feel entrenched, or even trapped. They begin to suffer different degrees of angst and dissatisfaction. Eventually their confidence is shaken and they begin to question their own sense of purpose. They lose sight of their "true north." Ultimately, they wonder whether they're cut out for the long, hard road to the pinnacle of corporate success.

Most of all, they wonder, *Why am I doing this? Is it worth it?*

ABOUT THIS BOOK

I wrote this book to help executives—or anybody who aspires to be one—navigate the turbulent waters inherent in working for a large corporation. Succeeding at the highest levels of a multinational company takes much more than just hitting your numbers each quarter. You also have to manage your emotions and the emotions of your team, understand the culture-within-a-culture, map out your stakeholders, set up a frequency schedule, lead by your actions, take your credit to the bank, overcome underwhelm, find your *why*, and avoid burnout. Whew! That seems like a lot, and it is. But these skills aren't optional. They are essential.

In this book, I share what I've learned over twenty-four years as an executive at marquis global corporations PricewaterhouseCoopers and GE. Think of the following eight chapters as the rules of the road for making it to the C-Suite. My goal is to empower you to succeed so you, too, can enjoy all the fruits of being a senior corporate leader. I will pull no punches in pointing out the complications and conundrums of corporate life, while also celebrating the corporate world and inspiring readers to find their happiness and success within it.

Corporate life does not come with a "how to navigate" manual. There are really two ways to understand these essential lessons—either spend a decade or two in the trenches and earn your scars, or read this book. I suggest the latter. I've already done the hard part for you. All you have to do is absorb it.

So, turn the page and let's accelerate your journey to the highest levels of corporate leadership.

CHAPTER 1

THE LION AND THE GOAT

"A lion never loses sleep over the opinion of a goat."
—ADAPTED FROM A QUOTATION BY VERNON HOWARD

There are two types of people in this world: lions and goats. Which one would you like to be? The lesson in this chapter is an important concept for any aspiring corporate executive to fully understand.

SAFARI ANIMALS

When tourists travel halfway around the world to go on safari, what do they want to see? Which animal is at the top of their list? Usually it's the lion. When they show pictures of their trip to friends back home, the first question they hear is, "Did you see any lions?" All the big game animals in Africa are popular—elephants, giraffes, rhinos, hippos, and so on. But the lions always seem to draw the most attention and awe. In fact, if you come home without having seen a lion, you'll almost certainly be disappointed with your entire trip.

Why is that?

Perhaps it's because people on an open-top jeep safari know that a lion could easily become aggressive if it wanted to. Seeing a lion in the wild is a brush with danger. That may be a factor, but I don't think it's the main reason people are fascinated by lions; there are many animals in the wild that can kill you. I think our admiration of lions goes deeper than that.

Lions represent something bigger, something grander. Lions are regal. They fear nothing. They're powerful, yet poised. They don't back down from a fight, even against a Cape buffalo that weighs two thousand pounds. Lions don't put up with nonsense from anyone or anything. They stand their ground. They have strength, wisdom, prowess, maturity, and total confidence. Yet they also show leadership, tenderness, and compassion toward other members of their pride, especially young lion cubs.

Can you tell I'm a big fan of lions? Perhaps it's because Africa is my home. There is much lore and legend around lions across the African continent. As the undisputed king of the sub-Saharan savannah, they've been revered as a symbol of strength for thousands of years.

Now, let's talk about the goat.

I think I just heard you chuckle. It's okay, I understand. After all, comparing the regal lion with the pedestrian goat is laughable, right? The two could not be more different. But in the comparison, we can learn much about how to act in corporate life.

The goat is perhaps best known around the world for being delicious in stews and kebabs, or in my favorite goat dish, biryani. Goats are prey. They're not particularly talented at anything except appearing on a dinner table.

But my problem with goats is more than that. While goats can be light on their hooves and adeptly scamper up rocky mountain paths, they're also restless and flighty. They get scared easily, then run away quickly. They're fickle-minded, indecisive, and poor decision makers. They follow the herd. They never stand up for themselves, even if they're in a large group.

Let's compare these two animals in two different pressure situations. On Kenyan game preserves, it's sometime necessary to relocate a male lion from one area to another. The park rangers will surround the animal and then shoot it with a tranquilizer gun. Although outnumbered, the lion never shows fear. Even when being shot with multiple painful darts out of a high-powered rifle, and probably thinking it's going to die, the lion keeps its head held high. It never lowers its head in defeat. Unlike a frightened dog, the lion doesn't bark, yip-yap, or squeal. It always projects confidence and strength, no matter how bleak things may look.

In contrast, the goat gives in without even putting up a fight. I lived in Iran as a child, which had a festival each year called *Eid al-Adha*; in English it means "feast of the sacrifice." When the festival goers would get ready to sacrifice a goat, or *bakri*, the goat would sense what was coming, put its head down, and accept its fate without protest or struggle. It didn't even try to fight.

Compare the two. The lion holds its head high with defiance and pride. The goat bows its head in surrender. They're clearly very different animals with completely different DNAs.

THINK LIKE A LION

I want readers of this book to think and act like a lion in the corporate world. Never act like the goat. When faced with a challenge, a pressure situation, or even imminent defeat, hold your head high. Know that you are strong and resilient, and that you will bounce back and end up on top, once again.

I taught my now-ten-year-old daughter, Bianca, about the lion and the goat years ago. I was never more proud than the first time I saw her implement the lesson.

When Bianca was nine years old, she was having trouble with a bully at school. She came home visibly upset one day after the bully was mean to her. Instead of going to her room and crying (goat behavior), she asked my wife for her telephone. Bianca told us she wanted to call the bully's mother and ask her to make him stop.

I told my wife to dial the number and give the phone to Bianca. *Let's see what happens*, I thought. When the boy's mother answered, Bianca calmly and with poise, even though she was upset, spoke to her: "Hello, Aunty, this is Bianca. Your son has been mean to me at school. I'm not complaining. I don't want to get him in trouble, but he has been mean to me for a few weeks and it's actually troubling me a lot; it's not nice, and I would like it to stop. Can you please help me?"

I was just amazed by that. It was classic lion behavior. She didn't bark, or yip-yap, or raise her voice. She wasn't aggressive or even confrontational. But she made it clear that she was not going to take that kind of nonsense from anyone, especially a bully. She stood tall, stood her ground, and dealt with the problem head-on. It was clear she wasn't going to back down. I don't know too many nine-year-olds who are mature enough to have a direct and honest dialogue to solve a pressing problem for themselves. My little lion!

NO ONE WANTS TO BE A GOAT

Everyone understands that it's better to be the lion than the goat. But not everyone can be a lion. How many people truly have the fortitude and the courage to do it? It takes all the lion characteristics I spoke of earlier, plus one more important one—restraint.

You might be aware that, of all the animals in the animal kingdom, the lion is one of the quietest. They're apex predators. They're almost entirely silent. Being a lion means you never have to roar, never have to get aggressive or in-your-face with people. You remain calm and confident, even in the face of overwhelming challenges or certain defeat. Like the lion, you only roar if you absolutely have to.

Take the United States Navy SEALs, for example. These special forces troops go through the toughest training in the world. No matter how difficult the training gets, they teach the SEALs to act like lions. I once watched a video of a US Navy officer giving a talk about SEAL training. He told a story of how they take the cadets out into the ocean off Southern California and dump them into shark-infested waters. He said, "We tell our cadets that as these sharks swim around you, be strong, maintain your focus, and keep moving toward your goal. If the shark gets too close and you think that it's about to bite you, punch him in his nose. Otherwise, keep your head down, swim hard, and stand your ground." Maybe the US Navy should call them the Navy LIONS.

Many people have compared the corporate world to swimming with sharks. It can be scary at times. But the rewards are worth it. If you're not up for it, remember: not everyone has to be a lion. The world needs goats, too, and we all love a good biryani!

A LION IN THE CONFERENCE ROOM

As a corporate leader, or someone who soon will be, you would be well-served to step into the business archetype of the lion. Show a lion's courage, strength, confidence, and endurance. Think of yourself as a powerful lion, never a skittish goat. It will be reflected in how you carry yourself and how you act in the office, in meetings, and with clients. It will influence how others perceive you, both in and out of the office. It will help you to overcome challenges and adversity and to keep your head held high. No matter what goes wrong, you will always remain strong, poised, and in control. Modeling the lion is one of the keys to a long and prosperous corporate career.

You'll meet all kinds of negative people in your career, from backstabbers to complete jerks. You'll experience obstructionists who want nothing more than to build walls in front of you and block your path. But if you maintain the characteristics discussed above, they will eventually realize who is the lion and who is the goat. They'll treat you accordingly. In my experience, the world steps around you as it experiences you. Go through this world as a lion.

A lion is powerful, but only flexes its ample muscles when absolutely necessary. Overusing your strength when not required can be damaging to your reputation, and to others. For example, an executive who is a lion would never berate a subordinate in front of colleagues, or even raise his voice unless there were no other options. Even then, a true lion would find another way to stay regal and dignified, while still getting the point across. Lions are not condescending to waitstaff in restaurants, they don't treat housekeeping with disrespect, they're polite and respectful to flight attendants, and they never raise their voice or get aggressive, no matter how poor the service may be. They almost always use a light touch, while making it clear they won't tolerate nonsense from anyone. Goats can be noisy, they bleat (which sounds like the cry of a human baby), they scamper in haste, and they always back down. Lions do not.

THOMAS THE LION

My friend Thomas is a good example of being a lion in the corporate world. Thomas rose up through the ranks over twenty-plus years at GE. He has a fantastic pedigree, top-shelf education, deep operational experience, and a succession of bigger and bigger jobs. About ten years ago, he left GE for a while to take on another venture. When he came back to GE several years later in a CFO role, he ran into some turbulence.

Some within the finance fraternity viewed his absence as a gap in his financial function, and they discounted whatever he might have accomplished on the outside. They treated him, at first, almost as an outsider in what was a very insider role as CFO. Thomas also found he had some stakeholder misalignments and misunderstandings, which was a problem for someone in such a senior role.

Altogether, some of his new coworkers were not giving him his due respect. They seemed to have sharp elbows around him. They had their daggers out, and Thomas felt like he had a large target on his back.

But what Thomas's new colleagues didn't know was that Thomas is a lion. He held his head high and persevered with grit and determination. Thomas had the fortitude and courage to stand up and confront these issues head-on. But he didn't shout, complain, protest, or make a scene. Thomas didn't raise his voice or get aggressive. He didn't pull the title card and demand respect. He didn't complain to his superior. That's not what lions do. He knew he could handle it on his own. He is a lion.

Thomas stood his ground, showed courage in the face of adversity, and didn't back down. He made it clear he wouldn't put up with any nonsense. Eventually, he came out on top and stronger than ever. People respected him for his restraint in dealing with the situation, and for his grit and determination. He never roared, but he showed his strength.

Today, almost six years later, Thomas is sharing his lion strength with the rest of his pride. He is a respected mentor to many young African business leaders. A lot of people look up to him and admire him greatly, including coworkers who might have been obstacles at the outset. Thomas has his pride's back.

BULLDOZERS DON'T MAKE MANY FRIENDS

Many young corporate executives who don't know any better make a classic and highly avoidable mistake. They may have lionlike traits, but they're misguided about the use of them. They leverage their power in an unfortunate way—I call it the display of power.

Others have called it being a bulldozer. These terms refer to when an executive uses his office, title, or mandate to demand that they get their way. Often, this results in the use of bullying, job threats, or intimidation to silence resistance, alternate viewpoints, or any other behavior that is not to their liking. It is a form of head-to-head industrial conflict where the more senior person knows he's going to prevail solely due to his position above the subordinate.

The reason this is unfortunate is because being a bulldozer doesn't work in the long term. It may achieve its goal in the short term; but, over time, this tactic doesn't create loyal team members and subordinates. It alienates them.

Lions never use the bulldozer technique. They know they

don't have to. They understand that the damage it causes is often more detrimental than the benefit.

RANGE ROVER SPORT VERSUS TOYOTA PROBOX

Let me illustrate with an example. You are perhaps familiar with the Range Rover Sport, a luxury vehicle manufactured by Jaguar Land Rover. However, you may not know that in most developing countries, Toyota sells an inexpensive five-seater station wagon called the Probox. The Range Rover is obviously a super-premium luxury SUV built like a tank. The Probox is sort of the opposite. It's an inexpensive, cheaply built tin box on wheels. Look it up to see what one looks like.

If a Range Rover were in a head-on collision with a Probox, the Probox would suffer much more visible damage. The Range Rover would likely take out the entire front, including the radiator of the Probox. Meanwhile, the Range Rover would only suffer a fender bender or, at best, a damaged bumper. It would therefore appear that the Range Rover was the winner of that frontal encounter, right?

Wrong.

Eventually, the owner of the Range Rover will take it in to the dealer to have it repaired. He'll find out that even though he seemingly suffered less damage in the head-to-head collision, the cost of repair is actually much higher. The repairs to the seemingly minor damage to the Range Rover will be more costly than replacing the radiator and front chassis of the Toyota.

Using this metaphor, I often coach executives, teams, and mentees not to get into a head-to-head conflict. Don't go frontal into a head-on collision with a colleague or, especially, a subordinate. Even if you win the encounter, the damage you sustain will be far greater because it hurts your reputation and career longevity. The cost of a head-to-head conflict with a colleague is steep, and the self-inflicted damage is hard to overcome.

I know this is hard for type A, hard-charging, aggressive young executives to accept. It was for me too. I made plenty of these mistakes early in my career, before I learned to be a lion. Executives who pick fights with secretaries or junior people, lean hard on new hires, speak sharply to interns, use expletives in meetings, throw fits, get angry, slam doors—all those behaviors that show their anger—are doing themselves no favors. Those behaviors end up costing them dearly over time because people are watching. In the corporate environment, people are always watching.

So be a lion. Be powerful. But never abuse that power.

A CULTURE-WITHIN-A-CULTURE

For the first ten years of my career, I was living on the East Coast of the United States—first in Washington, DC, then in New York City, and finally settling in Boston. I worked as an infrastructure specialist with Pricewater-houseCoopers (PwC). As such, I had a book of business overseeing infrastructure deals, mostly in Eastern Europe, Russia, Asia, and Latin America. But at that time there was a region of the world where infrastructure growth was accelerating rapidly, and PwC wanted me to relocate there.

AN EPIC ADVENTURE

PwC asked me to move to Kenya. They wanted me to work

throughout the sub-Saharan region. The partners wanted me to help build a project and infrastructure finance practice based out of the Nairobi office. I'd never lived in Africa before, but it sounded like a great career move—not to mention an epic adventure. Instead of taking red-eye flights out of Boston to Central America or Asia, I would be flying to Lagos, Nigeria; Accra, Ghana; Dar es Salaam, Tanzania; and Johannesburg, South Africa. I was up for it.

I figured moving to Africa and adjusting to life in Nairobi would be a significant challenge. There would be new culture, languages, people, customs, and plenty of lifestyle adjustments. The part I anticipated would be easiest was joining the team in the Nairobi office of PwC. I was an experienced leader in my field; they were a nascent infrastructure team. It should be a perfect fit, and I thought we would be off to the races in no time.

That's not what happened.

NEW HIRES IN A NEW ENVIRONMENT

When I relocated to Kenya, the PwC Nairobi office was in expansion mode. They wanted to make some big bets in the region. The partners had determined that infrastructure was going to be a growth area, so they hired me. Around that same time, they also hired a mergers and acquisitions (M&A) specialist from South Africa, and a tax specialist from Australia. The South African M&A guy had never worked for PwC or for a Big Four firm. The Australian tax guy came from Ernst and Young, so he had Big Four experience. All three of us were hired as non-equity directors. Even though I came from PwC, I still considered myself a new hire.

Early on, all three of us felt a little out of place. We weren't fully accepted by our teams, so we'd get together and talk about this, since all of us were feeling the same way. We felt our experience was discounted, in a way. We felt like outsiders who didn't have the trust of our teams. Even though the partners had brought each of us in to do a job, none of us felt that we had their full backing.

I soon realized that the Nairobi office—and my infrastructure team in particular—was a *culture-within-a-culture*. Even though they were part of the same large company, their office and teams had a unique personality. They had their own corporate culture, their own characters in the office, and their own distinct way of doing things. I hadn't earned their trust or acceptance yet, so I wasn't seen as part of the team.

I knew what I had to do. First, I had to stop spending so much time with the other two new hires, and instead spend time bonding with my infrastructure team. I realized that going to lunch every day and socializing outside of work with the other new hires was sending the wrong message to my team. It was making the problem worse. I knew I had to integrate and go deeper with them, learn from them, and earn their trust. So that's what I did; and I really worked hard at it.

The South African M&A guy and the Australian guy didn't do that. They both continued to hang out mostly with each other. The M&A director, in particular, remained aloof and isolated from his team. He never earned their trust, he didn't show a willingness to learn from them, he wasn't seen as paying his dues, and he built a wall of isolation around himself. As a result, his team never fully accepted him or trusted him. He was an outsider, and that hindered his ability to be effective. He was the first casualty of the culture-within-a-culture, and he left the firm in less than a year.

The Australian guy lasted longer, but he too eventually became a victim of the culture-within-a-culture. He had success at PwC from a functional standpoint, but he failed to integrate into his team. He was never seen as having their backs, so they never had his. He didn't work hard to earn their trust. Two years in, he was passed over for partnership, so he left.

I took a different approach. I worked really hard to become part of my team and to get to know my peers and the partners. I recognized the culture-within-a-culture and spent a lot of time trying to overcome it. Ultimately, I was able to integrate into my team, earn their trust, learn from them, and have their backs. In return, they had mine. After two years, I made partner.

Through hard work, and by recognizing the challenges of a culture-within-a-culture, I was able to overcome being the new guy.

HOW AND WHY YOU BECOME THE NEW GUY OR WOMAN

I moved seven thousand miles around the world from Boston to Nairobi. That international move was a pretty dramatic setup for becoming a new guy. In most instances, however, becoming the new guy or woman happens much more subtly than that. It also happens to executives more frequently than we might realize. In fact, in any successful corporate career, an executive often has to start over in a new situation, complete with new people and new surroundings.

This common experience can happen when making a move to a new city, as I did, or making a lateral move within the same company when an executive is transferred to a new role, albeit a more senior position. Of course, any time you join a new company you're automatically the new person.

Being the new guy or woman involves a number of challenges for senior leaders. There's a subculture that must be navigated and, in many ways, overcome. The executive has to start over.

As my career progressed and I grew wiser and more experienced, I understood that all large corporations have their own subcultures. Even the most experienced senior executive cannot escape the culture-within-a-culture phenomenon they'll encounter whenever they become the new guy or woman.

Since you're an ambitious executive, you will eventually experience these challenges too. You'll feel isolated from your new colleagues, rather than included. You'll get frustrated trying to navigate the subculture-within-a-subculture. You'll be an outsider—at least for a while.

A STARK CONTRAST

When you join an existing team, you'll naturally be viewed with a heavy dose of skepticism until you earn their trust, which takes time. This is human nature. You're seen as an outsider because you weren't groomed or promoted from within. You don't have shared experiences with the existing team. You haven't lived in the trenches and fought the battles along with them. You're an unknown quantity.

AUTHOR'S NOTE: NEW GUY, NEW WOMAN, OR NEW PERSON

You'll notice that I alternate between writing *new guy* or *new woman* and *new person* throughout this chapter. It might be a bit cumbersome, but I want this book to be inclusive of all audiences. I do not want to exclude any reader based on gender.

Over the course of my career, I've had the privilege and pleasure to work with and for many amazing and talented women. For example, my first boss at PwC was a tough Cuban-American woman partner, and I learned so much from her. While the strategies and information in this book are equally effective for executives of both genders, I also recognize that there is an additional layer of complexity and nuance that women executives must navigate and manage throughout their corporate careers. Being a man, I realize that I can't begin to address the topic without sounding patronizing. There are also dozens of excellent books and resources on the topic of women in leadership, beyond what this book will encompass. So, let me just say here that I authentically respect and am genuinely grateful for the tremendous contributions that women mentors and executives have made in my career, and I hope this book can help many more talented women executives rise to the top of corporate life.

What makes this experience so uncomfortable is the contrast with your previous position. You used to be a key team member. Your colleagues looked up to you. They asked you for advice—both personally and professionally. You were a leader. You socialized with everyone and were invited to every party, lunch, dinner, and to drinks. You were tapped into the network. But, in this new role, you're not even part of it.

It's only natural that you'll feel excluded. *Why aren't they including me? I'm the leader, why aren't they coming to me with problems or solutions? Why wasn't I invited to the bar after work?*

It's lonely. It's uncomfortable. It's like a trial by fire, and you have to either navigate it successfully or suffer the consequences.

But I promise you, it is possible to overcome being the new guy or woman. I did it, and so have many of my mentors, mentees, and friends.

MY FRIEND VINNY!

When my buddy, Vinny, became the new person, he was an experienced investment banker. He was well known in Wall Street circles, and he was well respected. He had twenty years of experience, an MBA from Wharton, and an impressive career trajectory.

After a few down years during the recession, Vinny took a more senior position at a European investment bank. He was doing basically the same job in the same business. He was overseeing the same clients, doing the same work every day, and was in an office just a few blocks away from his old office. But it was a completely different work environment.

Vinny was now the new guy in a culture within the larger Wall Street culture. He was now working for a European investment bank, instead of an American investment bank. Even though Vinny had been through the trenches and closed dozens of deals with his previous firm, he hadn't been through anything with his new team. They didn't know him, so they didn't trust him.

It took Vinny many months of hard work getting to know the team, putting out fires together, having their backs, and proving himself before he earned their trust. He also focused on getting to know the individuals on his team and understanding their stories, their background and education, their connections and mutual acquaintances. He learned where their spouses worked, how old their children were, where they grew up, and what their hobbies were.

"It's kind of like speed dating," Vinny told me. "I have a limited amount of time to learn as much about them as possible." Spending the needed time was incredibly helpful to Vinny because he could then talk to them in a meaningful way that resonated with them.

Plus, Vinny had a huge advantage that most people don't have: he was able to bring some of his old team with him to the new bank. He already had a loyal crew he could count on to help him deliver results. But he was still the new person on the team for quite some time, until he earned his way in.

DENIAL DOESN'T WORK

The first step in learning to navigate your new-guy status in the culture-within-a-culture is to recognize it for what it is. The first time you find yourself in this position, you'll experience an uneasiness—you'll feel like something is off. *I was highly respected in my previous job, but I don't feel that way here. What's up?*

After a short time, you're likely to do what I did and question whether these feelings are valid. *I've never been treated this way. Is it just my imagination? Is it the team? Is it me? Have I changed? Is it my fault?* You might try to *deny* that your new colleagues are treating you differently than

the other team members, or you may try to sim
discussing it or thinking about it.

But you need to face it. Those feelings you're _____
are real.

Denial doesn't work. Neither does inaction, repression,
or avoidance. If you simply avoid dealing with the reality
of what's happening, then the problem will likely persist.
The level of mistrust is real, and it influences how others
interact with you.

But don't take it personally. The mistrust is not because
of anything you did. Your new team members still don't
know you or what a high-quality person you are. To them,
you're simply seen as an outsider who's not yet part of the
team. Trust takes time.

WHAT CREATES MISTRUST

Every organization has its own established culture. This
culture includes working styles, office etiquette, meeting
protocols, personalities, relationships, cliques and alli-
ances, ways of working together, social patterns, lunch
routines, and so on. These established patterns are
familiar and comfortable. Any time a new person enters
the mix, there's a chance the established order could be

upset. This is especially true when there's a new person in leadership with the power to make changes—including personnel changes.

Be prepared to recognize the feelings of "new person syndrome." Don't think you're above it, and don't deny it. Deal with it directly using the strategies discussed later in this chapter.

Above all, never pull out the "I'm the boss" card. Don't ever demand a seat at the table because you have a fancy title and power. That doesn't inspire subordinates. It disenfranchises and infuriates them.

Don't think your fancy suits, corner office, corporate perks, reserved parking spot, and impressive title will make everyone instantly respect you and trust you. They won't. In fact, the opposite is true; the more seniority you flaunt, the more your team members will want to see you prove your worth. They won't be impressed until you deliver outcomes.

It's not uncommon for executives who graduated from prestigious colleges, business schools, or elite corporate training programs to assume they'll have an instant connection with their new colleagues. If they've shared values and similar experiences, they think the new team will be more likely to trust them. This is generally a false assumption. Being in the same college fraternity does not necessarily build trust.

There's no way around it. You'll have to walk through the fire and prove your battle skills in the trenches with the rest of the team, no matter what your title or pay grade is.

IMMERSE YOURSELF

When you find yourself as the new person, struggling with this culture-within-a-culture phenomenon, you'll wonder about the best way to get past it. How should you respond? You can't eliminate the breaking-in period, so what's the best way to get through this uncomfortable period as quickly as possible?

When I joined the Nairobi office of PwC, I spent quite a few sleepless nights wondering about misalignments and why I felt like an outsider. I felt some isolation at work, then worried about it at home until I realized what I had to do. I had to overcome the obstacles in the office by diving into the deepest part of the office culture, full-force.

I immersed myself in the culture-within-a-culture, addressing the problem with the same urgency and focus I would if I were going after a big piece of business. I met with my colleagues, set up lunches, and invited my team to client meetings. I scheduled myself to work and travel with them, and I attended events and conferences with them. I tried to learn as much as possible about all of the team members in my department.

In those early months, I worked hard to connect with my colleagues in a wide variety of settings. I got to know them, asked about their families and their lives, and sought to understand their goals and aspirations. I used the tried-and-true method of connecting with people by using immersion and my emotional IQ to navigate the new team and the new situation.

MONITOR THE INTERNAL TWITTER

Once I immersed myself in my team, I realized they had a false impression of me. They had heard I was "an investment banker from the States," so there might have been a preconceived perception that I was this "Wall Street type"—a big-talking, arrogant, and aggressive deal maker without much local empathy to African issues. That was unfair, because I had spent my career working almost exclusively in emerging markets, albeit from the US. Most of these folks had not even interacted with me, so they didn't know me at all. I had to set the record straight.

Every office environment has what I call "internal Twitter." In other words, there's a rumor mill in every office, and it can't be ignored. You must proactively manage the chatter floating around about yourself in short order. Otherwise, these false or misleading assumptions might stick, attaching themselves permanently and hardening around you.

The benefit of immersing yourself is that you get the opportunity to change people's minds. I knew I had to find a way to subtly demonstrate that I was a team player—that I was hands-on, I was a thought leader in infrastructure, and I was empathetic to emerging markets. Those were the outcomes I needed in order to squash the negative and erroneous perception of me.

I knew that working on deals and putting points on the board goes a long way toward demonstrating one's skill and building credibility. Working closely with my team, we won clients, generated big fees, and developed people and the practice. They saw that I was always focused on outcomes. Through these efforts, the word got out. I turned the internal Twitter in my favor by deliberately and relentlessly counteracting it with the truth *and* with my actions.

Because of the results we delivered by working together,

my stakeholders no longer believed negative comments when they circulated around the internal Twitter. "Vishal is not like that. That perception is wrong." My team members stood up for me and had my back. Not only that, but they flooded the internal Twitter with *positive* tweets about me. They became my ambassadors and my allies, shooting down fake news about me and replacing it with positivity. This is the type of loyalty every leader should aspire to create.

Your network and alumni can be a great help when it comes to rebuilding credibility after a big move. Former classmates, colleagues, and team members who also transition to the new culture with you can help vouch for you. They can alert you if negative perceptions are floating around, and they are likely to be loyal since they've known you for a long time.

FIND YOUR COMPASS

While you're doing all the steps in this chapter and figuring out the new culture-within-a-culture, you don't have to do it alone. One of the best things you can do is find an internal mentor at the company. I call this finding your compass, because a wise mentor can point you in the right direction. Find someone more senior, but usually not your direct manager, and develop a social relationship with them. If you can find a coach in such a person, it can have tremendous value. Leverage your network, ask for recommendations, keep your eyes open, and find your compass.

GET TO KNOW YOUR TEAM

I put a lot of effort into learning about the team in a truly authentic way. *Where did they grow up? Where did they go to college? What motivates them? What are their goals and values? Are they young and single living with roommates, or married with children?* I tried to remember the names of those in their family and even meet them if I could. I remembered where their children went to school. I also studied their resumes, looking for common experiences and mutual acquaintances.

I made a point to speak with all team members regularly and slowly built relationships that were deeper than just being office acquaintances. I also used the strategies of frequent touchpoints, connectivity, sharing, and collaboration. I learned from them, and then incorporated some of those lessons going forward. They felt appreciated and valued.

Within about one year, I had built trust and respect. My team realized I was competent and experienced, and they appreciated that I cared enough to ask about them and their lives.

Eventually, I felt a shift. They now wanted to collaborate with me, ask for my advice, share strategies with me, and bounce ideas off me. They trusted me. They respected my opinions. Even though I came from far outside the Nairobi office, I was no longer an outsider.

If I had just ignored those feelings of isolation, and if I had ignored the internal Twitter, that false narrative could have stuck permanently. In many instances within a corporation, perceptions can become reality. You have to do the work to counteract false perceptions and rumors before they set permanently.

NO ONE WILL FOLLOW YOU JUST BECAUSE OF YOUR RESUME

You can't force team loyalty. Demanding it does not work. You can't ask your team members, "Have you heard anything bad about me lately?" That type of insecurity does not build confidence or trust.

You have to inspire your team authentically through truly being yourself, delivering outcomes, and sharing credit with your team selflessly. Otherwise, the negative internal Twitter is probably telling the truth about you. You can't battle the truth.

No one follows you just because you have an impressive resume. It takes more than just experience to be a leader. People follow you because they trust and believe in you.

They know you have their backs, and they've seen you in action with their own eyes. The very best way to build trust is by fighting battles together and having one another's back. When a group of people band together as a team to achieve a common goal, the experience builds camaraderie and fosters trust.

There is nothing that bonds people together more than going through an epic challenge by working together and then coming out on the other side. The more this happens, the stronger the bonds become. Spending years in the trenches together can often forge friendships and bonds that last a lifetime.

Fighting battles together helps foster closer bonds because of the hard work, intensity, and adrenaline involved in fighting for and closing big deals. This is why I always strategically look at my team members, staffers, and extended team to see who I want to invite into the trenches with me for a given deal. It makes sense to deliberately choose people you want to build stronger bonds with—to attend big meetings and work on deals. That way you both get a shared experience of working hard and winning together. It builds trust and respect.

I don't always take the same team members. I strategically look for new people I need on my side, and then invite them to work on deals with me. This helps my team and extended team members build their skills and gain experience, and it helps me forge stronger bonds with a wide range of stakeholders. It also reveals a lot about each team member. Who worked hard for the team? Who carried their own weight? Who contributed more than their fair share? Who was willing to make a personal sacrifice to win the battle?

By the way, wartime analogies for business are not as exaggerated as they might seem. Corporate life can feel like a battlefield. The accountability that shareholders and your own organization place on you is something you must take seriously in corporate life if you're going to be successful. Misses are rarely tolerated, and they're not easily forgiven.

Trust and respect cannot be ordered. You cannot demand that your team trust and respect you. You can't buy trust or respect from your local supermarket, no matter how much money you have. Trust is not something that automatically comes with a new job or promotion. It's not personal. Everybody has to go through their own rite of passage to earn it, invest in it, leverage it, harvest it, treasure it, and *share* it.

THE UNIFORM

I once learned a valuable lesson from a charismatic senior partner named Juan Carlos Acebal when I was a young intern at PwC in Washington, DC. I went to speak with him on behalf of the other interns. We were asking whether we could stop wearing business suits on Fridays during the hot and humid summer. We wanted to be able to dress down on "casual Fridays." Juan Carlos responded by saying, "How do you dress on the battlefield?" I replied, "In armor." He said, "That's right. On a battlefield, you don't stop wearing your armor just because it's Friday. Please don't come to work in anything but a suit."

Since then, I've worn a suit and a pair of cufflinks to work every day. This incident shaped my principles and became a permanent part of my value system. I always want to be properly dressed for battle, and I want my team to be as well. I once sent a team member home after he showed up at the office unshaven. This may be a bit anachronistic today, but I believe in the structured discipline and intensity of doing business, and I feel it's important to dress the part. I believe it impacts outcomes.

GIVE TO GET

ONE OF THE MOST IMPORTANT AND VALUABLE LESSONS I'VE LEARNED THROUGHOUT MY ENTIRE BUSINESS CAREER IS THAT YOU MUST GIVE TO GET. IF YOU WANT ACCEPTANCE AND TRUST AND ADMIRATION FROM YOUR TEAM, PEERS, BUSINESS ASSOCIATES, AND CUSTOMERS ALIKE, THEN YOU HAVE TO GIVE THEM YOUR ACCEPTANCE, TRUST, AND ADMIRATION, AND THE VERY BEST OF YOUR VALUABLE SKILLS. IF YOU WANT THEM TO DELIVER FOR YOU, THEN YOU HAVE TO DELIVER FOR THEM (FIRST).

FOR EXAMPLE, I AM ALWAYS THE FIRST TO SHARE MY CONTACTS AND MAKE INTRODUCTIONS—EVEN BEFORE SOMEONE ASKS ME TO. I'M THE FIRST TO DELIVER VALUE IN A BUSINESS RELATIONSHIP OR IN A DEAL. I'M ALWAYS EAGER TO SHARE VALUABLE INFORMATION AND INSIGHTS. I'M EVEN THE FIRST TO PAY THE DINNER BILL. I NEVER HOLD BACK FROM GIVING, AND I'M NEVER SHY TO MAKE THE FIRST MOVE TO OFFER VALUE. GIVING FIRST IS A GIFT TO YOURSELF, AND TO THOSE AROUND YOU. IT SETS YOU FREE. TRY IT AND SEE HOW IT OPENS DOORS FOR YOU.

Success in the corporate world is a long game. It takes time and effort. Even though corporate targets are short-term and demand immediate results in the current quarter, building relationships takes years. You can't cut loose and give up. You can't stop and say, "This isn't working for me." You have to keep at it and keep going.

And here's an added layer that makes all of this a bit more difficult: you will need to consistently do all of this while also meeting your numbers, budgets, outcomes, and everything else you were hired to do. You have to do all the relationship building on *overdrive*. It can be overwhelming to work hard all day to deliver numbers and then have to spend time outside the office building trust with your team. But if you want to be a senior leader, if you want to move up in the company, if you want to be successful, then you have to do the soft stuff too. In fact, you have to be *as good* at the soft stuff as you are at delivering your numbers and meeting your budgets; so the soft stuff is actually core stuff. You have to do both, and you have to do them well. The corporate world is not forgiving if you do either of them badly.

DON'T BE A SPA LEADER

Fighting in the trenches with the team is the opposite of what I call "spa leadership." You cannot be seen by your team as relaxing in the spa, getting a massage, and calling them from the sauna while they're in the trenches getting clobbered. A leader needs to be in the battle with his soldiers. Spa leaders never earn trust.

BEING THE NEW PERSON ISN'T EASY

I've observed, counseled, and mentored countless executives as they went through the same thing I described in this chapter. They were hired and brought into an office in a senior role, only to be excluded from the group because they were new. Many of them overcame these challenges. Others did not.

Being the new guy or woman isn't easy. In a way, you have to run through the gauntlet. It's a rite of passage. It's trial by fire, and not everyone makes it to the other side. But if you can make it through, you'll be better for it. Not only that, but you'll be one of the team.

NEW PERSON VERSUS BULL'S-EYE SYNDROME

I want to draw a clear distinction in this discussion of new person syndrome. If you're an executive and you get transferred to a new location or department, or you make a lateral move to a different employer, then you're the new person, because you're now working with all new faces. But if you're promoted within your own department, you're not the new person. Everyone already knows you. Even though you're in a new role, you are not an unknown quantity.

However, when you get promoted within your company, you have a new challenge to deal with. I call it "bull's-eye syndrome." There is a theory in management that every manager has a bull's-eye on their back, and their coworkers in the ecosystem around them (especially the junior coworkers) are gunning for them. When someone gets promoted to be a manager for the first time and they now supervise others, they're suddenly a target. When that person gets promoted to a more senior level of management, the bull's-eye gets bigger. I've never thought of senior leaders, C-Suite teams, and CEOs as having a bull's-eye on their backs—small or large. Rather, they are completely painted from head to toe as one giant bull's-eye!

You have to pay your dues. You have to build relationships. You have to show a willingness to learn, collaborate, and listen. Project an attitude that you're there to observe and work together as one of the team and to understand how the company works. You have to demonstrate a capacity for empathy and understanding.

You also have to keep your word and follow through on what you say you're going to do. This demonstrates that you're worthy of people's trust. You have to truly earn that over time. It doesn't matter what the headlines in the newspapers said about you, and it doesn't matter what's on your resume. Your resume is why you were hired into the position, but it won't help you beyond that.

It's also essential to have the backs of anyone who reports to you directly. They need to know you'll support them and back them up if they need you. The attitude of a leader should be, "I have your back." You have to be willing to shield your team from blame and supply sufficient air cover so they can deliver on the ground. If your team sees you take the heat for them, that builds respect and goodwill.

Overcoming new person syndrome in a culture-within-a-culture takes hard work, self-awareness, action, and immersion. Take matters into your own hands. Don't leave your reputation to chance. Monitor the internal Twitter feed in your office. Invest in learning about your team members, and endeavor to win them over with your actions.

A common theme in this book is that it is crucial to have stamina. You have to possess the endurance to go the distance. It took me almost a full year to overcome the new person syndrome and come out a winner on the other side. You must have the stomach for it—the steely determination to be the new guy or woman for a while. Eventually, you'll win.

At some point in your career, you may also experience the new person syndrome from the *other* side. That is, you may be part of an existing team when a new executive comes in to take over leadership of the team and she becomes the new woman. When this happens, be conscious of the effects of new person syndrome. By using some of the skills you learned in this chapter, you can help settle and coach the new person into her new role. If you do that, everyone will benefit.

A PRICELESS ASSET

So much depends on your reputation that you must guard it with your life. It's the most priceless asset you have in a corporate environment. Your reputation is the cornerstone upon which your career is built. This is why I counsel all executives to be keenly aware of any assault on their reputation, and to mitigate it immediately. I like to say that the only thing I take home to dinner with my family every night is my reputation.

STEP ON THE ACCELERATOR

Make sure the soft stuff gets done well by *accelerating* the soft skills. Apply the techniques in this chapter, and then step on the gas. Approach the culture-within-a-culture and your new-guy status with the same intensity that you do the rest of your job, because it really is just as important.

If you're reading this book, you are probably intense and focused on delivering key results. You have ambition, intensity, and urgency when going after your goals. Now you need to bring those same qualities to your soft skills of building trust, forging relationships, understanding the culture, and earning respect.

Succeeding at building these soft skills is the only way you can consistently deliver your numbers. The two are totally interconnected and interdependent. You have to build a team that works together, trusts one another, respects one another, and has one another's back, and you must act with urgency to condense the transition period as much as possible.

This is the most effective strategy for overcoming new person syndrome and succeeding in any culture-within-a-culture. But in addition to winning over your own team, you'll also have to work cross-functionally with people in other areas of the company. Chapter 3 lays out a specific strategy for "playing horizontal" within a company.

MAPPING OUT YOUR STAKEHOLDERS

In my twenty-four-year corporate career, I've had the honor of working for two huge, global corporations with complex operations around the world. As you can imagine, there are positives and negatives to working for a global behemoth.

Take GE for example. GE is a global industrial powerhouse with more than 330,000 employees serving customers in 180 countries. GE's key business units include healthcare, aviation, energy connections, power generation, renewable energy, oil and gas, rail transportation, and capital. That's quite a mix.

One of the challenges for GE is—and has always been—what the corporate world calls "playing horizontal": in other words, being able to coordinate people from different divisions to work cross-functionally and synergistically in order to maximize returns for shareholders.

It's not easy, but it can have a dramatic impact on the bottom line when it works. Therefore, most big corporations promote this idea of one team, one firm, one service provider. They advocate playing horizontal, and they discourage the silo mentality where each division works in isolation from the other divisions of the same company.

Over the course of my corporate career, I had a front-row seat to watch how this played out in practice. The reality: though evangelized by the corporate culture, playing horizontal in a huge corporation is difficult. The messaging and the vision might promote it, but the real world doesn't always work that way.

PLAYING HORIZONTAL IN THE REAL WORLD

At PwC, for instance, in my position as a deals partner, it was my job to pull people together from multiple disciplines. For example, on a typical project I might need someone from audit who specializes in media and tele-communications, someone from tax, someone from government affairs, and maybe someone from consulting who really knows operations. Delivering a large, multidimensional piece of work for any client is rarely a siloed process. It takes the effort of many people from different parts of the company.

Yet playing horizontal was a constant uphill battle. Playing horizontal requires one to be selfless. Individuals can be preoccupied by their silos, their mandates, and their P&Ls—in return, they often forget the needs of the end user or client, or the larger value to the company. I found it odd that even though we all worked for the same company and shared the same overall responsibility for profit and loss, we didn't share the same sense of urgency or priorities. I also found that if I was pulling a deal together and a team member from a different business was only a small fraction of that effort, then they would only feel a small amount of urgency. In other words, individual priorities of the various silos took precedence over broader organizational priorities. I began to question whether the organization's stated values truly translated into action on the part of the organization's leaders.

I hated that discrepancy. It flew in the face of this whole notion of playing horizontal, and it reduced the overall operating results of the company. It didn't make sense to me. At first, I thought this reluctance to work cross-functionally was caused by corporate structure. I wondered, *Why does this company give so much lip service to playing horizontal, but then, when the time comes, no one delivers?*

GO HORIZONTAL YOURSELF

After experiencing this disappointment more than a few times at different companies, and after talking to friends who work at other large corporations, I realized this was a very common experience in the corporate world. Many large companies pride themselves on their ability to play horizontal, but few live up to the vision. As a result, senior executives naturally feel anxiety over this gap between expectations and reality.

Furthermore, I realized this anemic ability to work cross-functionally isn't necessarily caused by anything built into the corporate structure. It's caused by *individuals*, and you'll need those individuals on your side to succeed. Gaining the support from people in the different silos will require some of the same skills we talked about in chapter 2: building trust, forging relationships, understanding expectations, and giving to get.

I determined that the most efficient and reliable way to play horizontal was for me to go horizontal *myself*. This was nonnegotiable. The company wasn't going to do it for me. I had to be the one to make it happen.

I decided to reach out and build my own relationships with the individuals in the various silos. I employed many of the same skills detailed in chapter 2, including connecting with individuals professionally and socially, and attacking this problem with urgency and focus.

THE STAKEHOLDER MAP

I created something that became a tremendous asset, which I call a "stakeholder map." I am an outcomes-driven person, and in order for me to live the values of the organization and deliver across silos, I needed to map out my stakeholders in a structured ecosystem to better understand the organization and the individuals within it.

Why is a stakeholder map important? The stakeholder map allows me to create a playbook of how to navigate my way around the company ecosystem, helping me play across the board. It empowers me to break through any culture-within-a-culture and know which path to take when I'm in difficulty. It also keeps me focused on building relationships with the people who are key to my success.

Once I have my stakeholder map built, I have to give it

attention every day, working toward building relationships and trust with the people in those other silos. You have to *Give to Get*.

WHO ARE THE STAKEHOLDERS?

The ongoing success of every person in the organization is dependent on a network of key figures. You may not know who all of these people are in the beginning; but as you meet them and learn what piece of the business is in their control, you add them to the stakeholder map.

Start by examining your long-term goals in the company and in your career, and then identify the people who can help you achieve those goals. These people will be from many different silos within the company, including but not limited to operations, finance, legal, and government affairs. Each person on your map is someone you must rely on or work with from time to time to drive results, which makes them all key to your success.

The people on your stakeholder map will not only be executives or high-level decision makers. Some will be internal customers. Some may be midlevel or lower-level managers in different departments who don't report to you. Some will not be employees at all and will reside outside of the corporate structure.

The one common denominator is that you must rely on each of them in some way in order to achieve your desired outcomes. Think of it this way: if someone can delay your project, derail your timetable, influence the resources you require to drive your outcomes, affect the supply chain or the enablers that are required to support your objectives, that person should be considered a stakeholder. Stakeholders come in all sizes, from big to small. You'll be surprised how it's often the smallest stakeholder who can hold up the biggest projects. Don't overlook anyone you might need.

Everyone who fits this description should be added to your list. Literally create a list of names on your computer, adding a few notes on each person. You will use this list to draw your stakeholder map.

Notate next to each person whether they are a supporter of yours, a detractor, or an influencer. Supporters can be relied on to always have your back. Detractors can be relied on to always stab you in the back. Influencers should never be underestimated; even administrative staff can influence their managers.

CREATING THE MAP

Once you collect a list of key people, I want you to literally sketch out your map on a piece of paper (or on the computer) to create your own personal stakeholder organizational chart. Add the names and notes, and you can even add pictures of the key people if you like.

First, create a map of your inner circle, which should include all the senior decision makers from the different silos within the company. Then broaden the map to include the outer circle of influencers and other personnel who help the key decision makers. Also include anyone within the company who might be important from a visibility standpoint.

Finally, add all the external key people who don't work in the company, but who can have a direct impact on results. These people could include partners at an outside law firm, government officials, key suppliers, clients, or other influential advisors and outside decision makers.

FILLING IN THE MAP

As soon as you have written the names on the stakeholder map, it's time to do the important work. You will now focus on building relationships and trust with all of the people on your map. Start by scheduling face time with them, then build in some touchpoints at regular intervals to build and strengthen those relationships. Your goal is to forge bonds with all of your stakeholders, building a team of internal and external supporters.

When I took on a senior role at GE, I worked hard at building my stakeholder map. I made a list of all the key people whose help and support I would need. I drew my map, and then I went on a mission to get to know each of them as well as possible. I wanted to understand the ecosystem. I had more than one hundred names on my stakeholder map.

I organized what I called my "listening tour." I physically went out and met face-to-face with a wide selection of people. I reached out to them by email and over the phone and asked for a meeting. I simply said: "Hey, Mr. General Council, I want to learn more about your part of the organization, and understand some of what you're seeing. Can we meet?"

I set up dozens of meetings, and I even openly told people I was on a listening tour. If I couldn't meet with someone in person, we arranged a call by phone or videoconference. Most people will not view this request as a nuisance. On the contrary, they'll appreciate that you want to listen to what they have to say.

My listening tour was one of the smartest things I did at

GE. It helped me learn the issues, the key personnel, and the ecosystem. I strongly suggest you create a stakeholder map, and then go on a listening tour to fill in as many details as possible about each person.

When you do, keep your questions simple. Ask about their background. Understand what's important to them. Learn about their education, family, and career history. What have they encountered previously in their career that informs their decision making today? Strive to make it a conversation, never an interview. Look for common ground or mutual acquaintances. Understanding their impressions of your role, what they have experienced before, and what they would like to see differently from you and your role should always be a key part of the exercise.

Did I have plenty of extra time to do a listening tour? Of course not. I had a ton of regular work to do. My plate was overflowing. I had to deliver results. I had no time for polite conversation. But I made time, because these conversations were strategic and necessary. Don't skip this critical step. Don't lock yourself in your little office and refuse to pay attention to the world around you.

Also include in your map the connectivity between stake-holders. Who reports to whom? Who socializes with whom? Who doesn't get along with whom? This will help you understand how all these people are connected—to you and to one another.

THE NUMBER-ONE RULE OF A LISTENING TOUR

When conducting a listening tour, the natural tendency for most executives will be to talk about themselves. After all, you've done some pretty amazing things. Don't fall into this trap. The number-one rule of the listening tour is to ask questions *about the other person* and try to learn as much as you can about them.

You can talk about your own background and experience briefly, but refrain from reciting your resume. Everyone will already know your accomplishments simply because of the position you hold. Focus on the other person. They'll appreciate your interest in them. If you talk about yourself the entire time, you will have learned nothing new, and they may get the wrong impression about you.

USING THE MAP

Once you've created your stakeholder map and after you've met with each stakeholder, it's time to build some regular connectivity with them. This is essential. You have to figure out a routine or a schedule for regular touchpoints with each key stakeholder.

This could be a standing lunch every quarter with the CFO. It could be a monthly update meeting with government affairs. It could be a weekly call with each department head, or a standing Monday morning staff meeting.

The important point is to make it a routine and put it on the calendar. Don't just say, "Let's get together soon." That doesn't work. If you don't put it on the calendar, it won't happen. If you do put it on the calendar and something comes up, you can always cancel or reschedule.

Building connectivity through regularly scheduled touch-points is a key element of my management and leadership style. In conjunction with my stakeholder map, it has served me well.

Regardless of the size of your stakeholder map, establishing these rhythms is the best way to stay in the loop and stay connected with people. The key is to schedule consistent communication at regular intervals. Eventually this becomes a habit, so that you don't have to remember to keep the plants watered.

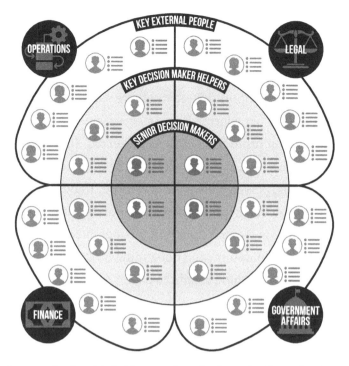

An example of a stakeholder map. Download an editable version from GivetoGetbook.com

HORSES FOR COURSES

Having regular contact is necessary, but it's not one-size-fits-all. Just as there are different horses for different courses, different stakeholders have different needs and prefer to connect in different ways. Some may want to meet you at the golf course; others may want to come to your office or have you come to theirs; still others will prefer to go have a drink after work. Every relationship requires a unique, personal touch.

That goes for frequency as well. With some people, such as your direct reports, it makes sense to have contact every week or even twice a week. For others, it makes sense to meet every month. There might be some people you see just once per quarter. Even once a year is better than nothing, but more frequently is preferred. In my most recent role at GE, I worked with people from healthcare, oil and gas, power, transport, and more. I saw the leaders of those businesses on some sort of rhythmic basis, depending on a combination of business needs from a frequency standpoint, and depending on the individual and the relationship I sought to have.

Establishing regular rhythms for such touchpoints is really important. It helps you to stay connected and keep information flowing. Having visibility helps keep you top of mind.

It's usually best to have some sort of agenda for each ongoing contact. Whether it's a call, a lunch, a Skype, or a meeting, I usually communicate two or three bullet points that I'd like to talk about. This little bit of structure makes these touchpoints more productive and efficient. It leaves more time for receiving and giving feedback, coaching, and mentorship.

As you get more and more seniority in a company, your

management role becomes more about being available to the team for guidance, problem solving, and driving the vision and values of your organization. It becomes critical to stay connected to the entire ecosystem, talking to them on a regular basis, problem solving, collaborating, and offering assistance. Sticking to a set rhythm of touchpoints with all my stakeholders was critical to my success—and I believe it served the stakeholders well too.

CORPORATE RETREAT COMING UP— HAVE YOU BOOKED YOUR MASSAGE YET?

Many executives view industry events and conferences as a chance to get out of the office, play some golf, take a break from the office, or just have fun. But I think these events are an ideal time to schedule multiple touchpoints with key people on your stakeholder map—or perhaps with people you'd like to add to your map.

When I attend a conference or a corporate getaway, I spend the two weeks prior setting up side meetings with key personnel. I get a list of attendees and compare that to my stakeholder map. Then at the conference, I might be having a whiskey with someone at the bar, but actually I'm spending time with that person because she's on my stakeholder map. As a result, my productivity and connectivity are sky high.

I strongly encourage you to do the same. Not doing this is a lost opportunity.

COMMUNICATE HARD DATA

Part of these regular touchpoints is communicating the hard data that needs to be shared with various stakeholders. The CEO may want to know where you are with certain projects. The CFO will want an update on when you expect revenue from certain projects. The department heads will also want this data.

The key here is to share the right amount of data with each stakeholder. Some people will want five pages of detailed financial information. Others will only want a one-sheet with a high-level overview of the numbers. Not everyone needs or wants the same depth and level of detail. While I encourage varying the quantity and depth for each stakeholder, I would always retain a standard approach to the headline numbers and messages for everyone.

It's always important to share standardized data. In other words, make sure the CFO, the CEO, and the department heads are all getting the same numbers. One stakeholder should never get outdated information while other stakeholders have more current numbers. In fact, I like using the same pages, the same sheets, and the exact same information, if possible.

Use your regular touchpoints to continually keep your stakeholders updated on key business metrics. They will appreciate feeling as though they're in the loop on all your projects, and you can use these touchpoints to build trust and rapport.

On the human side, they will feel they've been informed and included. Not to be corny about it, but this will make them feel that you care about their views. They'll feel you're respecting them, which is essential.

MAKE IT PERSONAL

Above all, remember to make each relationship on your stakeholder map a personal relationship. If all you do is talk about business strategy and spreadsheets, the relationship will remain a shallow one. You have to talk about family, friends, vacations, hobbies, spouses, children, and so on.

Making relationships personal makes them stronger and longer lasting. Relationships that are transactional tend to be one-dimensional and short-lived connections.

One way I've managed to personalize many professional relationships is through my love of food. I'm a foodie. I love fine dining and hospitality. I follow chefs from around the world on social media, know many personally, and love going to their restaurants when I'm in their city. I personally believe food and dining and good wine are great ways to bond people together. Sitting around a table, I can talk about food for hours; I've found food to be a common language for most. So, when I invite a stakeholder out to dinner, it often becomes a sharing and bonding experience.

I also love making restaurant suggestions. People call me all the time and say, "Hey, Vishal, I'm going to Beijing on business; where should I eat?" I will not only offer a suggestion, but I'll give them the chef's or restaurant manager's name, and I'll even call ahead and get them a table. Doing things like that really accelerates the relationship. *Give to Get.*

I happen to love food, but your thing could be football, cricket, Formula One, horses, fishing, sports cars, or any number of hobbies you can share with stakeholders. Inviting a stakeholder to a sporting event works well for many people. Find your *thing*!

BE A CONNECTOR OF PEOPLE

One of the best ways to *Give to Get* is to be a connector of people. As a senior executive, you have a valuable contact list. Use it to help people.

Let's say one of your stakeholders is trying to get a meeting at a big company, but they're not having any luck getting in. If you know someone there and you make a call on their behalf, or if you even set up the meeting, your value to that person will skyrocket. Unfortunately, most people tend to be stingy and protective of their networks. They often worry, *She will take over the relationship and leave me out.* I reject that notion, and I encourage you to be generous. Be a connector.

COFFEE TALK

Be sure to ask your stakeholders about their hobbies and interests. If someone is a connoisseur of coffee, for example, ask them for recommendations or take them to a new coffee shop in town for a coffee break. If you buy them a special coffee blend for their birthday or a holiday, imagine how much they will appreciate that you cared enough to remember what was important to them.

Always ask about children. People can talk about their children for hours. If you have children, you instantly have common ground.

Several years ago, my daughter dislocated her knee. It was a big deal in our lives. To this day, years later, I will never forget those who remembered and still ask me, "Hey, Vishal, how's Roshni's knee doing?" I can't tell you how special that makes me feel that they remembered. It all goes back to that important element of how someone makes you feel. I have no idea what business topic we were discussing then, but I will always remember how they made me *feel* when they asked about my daughter.

> *"I've learned that people will forget what you said, people will forget what you did, but people will never forget how you made them feel."*
>
> MAYA ANGELOU

That's how you connect with people on a personal level and build meaningful relationships. Taking an interest in people's personal stories and their lives moves the conversation away from being merely transactional. If I know your wife's name, or if I know that your dad is in hospital and ask about him the next time we see each other, or if I remember something else that is important to you, people remember that.

This is another form of *Give to Get*. You give the person the gift of remembering and caring about something important in their life. In return, they give you trust, loyalty, friendship, and respect. The more generous you are, the more you will receive in return.

No matter how you choose to do it, drawing people into some sort of genuine, humanistic dialogue is an important part of building relationships. No spreadsheet or quarterly report can ever supersede that, or be a substitute for it.

FEEDING THE REINDEER SOME SUGAR

Meeting regularly with stakeholders who work on your immediate team or in your office is pretty easy, right? You just ride the elevator or walk down the hall. Even if they work in an office five thousand miles away, you can still pretty easily connect with them through company functions, meetings, and email. As such, your immediate stakeholders aren't usually difficult to reach.

What about stakeholders who are further removed from you? Maybe you've identified your boss's boss as a key stakeholder. Or maybe it's someone in legal, or audit, or tax, or consulting, or someone in the C-Suite whom you don't see very much. If they're not on your team or in your immediate vicinity, they're probably not readily accessible to you, but they're an important stakeholder nonetheless. What do you do?

This is where the concept of *feeding the reindeer some sugar* comes in. Since you don't get face time with them on a regular basis, you've got to give them something to nibble on from time to time.

In other words, you have to give that stakeholder something to make them feel included. Indulge that person. Share something good with them. Send them new information they'll be interested in. Copy them on important emails. Bring them into the conversation. Make them feel like they're in the loop.

Feed that reindeer some sugar. It's a great way to keep the reindeer happy—and sugar is cheap.

PLAYING HORIZONTAL IS UP TO YOU

Leaders aspiring to grow into more senior leadership roles need to understand that the processes explained in this chapter are critical to their career success. A key point here: it doesn't come easy; it requires consistent effort over time.

To truly play horizontal in today's corporate world, you have to take charge of your own destiny. You can't rely on empty corporate platitudes. You have to build those horizontal relationships by hand.

Let me summarize. Identify the key cross-functional stakeholders whose help you'll need to make things happen, map the ecosystem, then wage a relentless charm offensive to build personal relationships and trust. Start by going on a listening tour. Really try to connect with each and every stakeholder on a personal level. Do all of this with the same sense of urgency that you bring to delivering your business results. Then accelerate the process. Dive deep and go all in. As I like to say, bring commercial intensity to make this happen. You have to take this into your own hands and be accountable for your own fate.

The last thing you want is to be viewed as siloed, as stuck in a vertical, as compartmentalized, or as part of a fiefdom. To move up in the company, you have to be viewed as someone who can work cross-functionally over many different verticals and with all types of people—both inside the company and out. You want to be seen as the leader who can play across the whole board.

ACTIONS ARE LOUDER THAN WORDS

For much of my corporate career I was a road warrior. Though, I suppose "air warrior" would be a more apt description. I was on at least two international flights each week, sometimes more. I spent more nights in hotel rooms in a year than most people do in a lifetime. It was hard on my family. My children would often say, "Dad *flies* to work on Monday mornings, as opposed to drives." It's nothing to be proud of, I must admit. They missed me when I was gone. I knew I had to maximize my time with them when I was home.

I also knew that anyone could talk a big game, but true leaders follow through on their promises and commitments with their actions. If I said to my wife, "I promise I'll make it up to you when I get back from this trip," I'd do everything I could to live up to that promise with my *actions,* no matter what.

After a grueling schedule while on a business trip to China, I hopped on a twenty-hour, long-haul flight from Beijing to Dubai to Nairobi. When I arrived home at 8:00 in the evening, I was completely wiped. Even though I was exhausted and running on fumes, I rallied, hopped in the shower, got dressed, and took my wife out to dinner and a movie. That was making sure my *actions spoke louder than words.*

In the past fifteen years, I haven't had a sip of alcohol on a flight for that very reason. I want to be alert and awake when I arrive at my destination—whether it's a date night with my wife, or a business meeting. Either way, I want to be sharp, present, and focused. I've never understood how some business travelers use international flights as an excuse to eat and drink to excess. If you stumble out of the airport hung over or dehydrated, how can you be at your best for whatever is waiting for you? *Actions speak louder than words.*

I also know that my wife, Mira, doesn't like to be reminded all weekend that I have to catch a flight on Monday morning. I understand that, so I go through the extra effort of never having a bag packed and waiting; I always store my luggage empty, put away, and out of sight. Even if I'm home for only a night or two in the middle of a killer week of travel, I completely unpack, and I'll bring Mira a thoughtful present from my travels. Even if I'm only at home for twenty-four hours, I want everyone to feel normal. The most valuable gift executives can give to their loved ones is not a designer-label outfit or luxury goods from the duty-free shop; it's the gift of their time.

IF YOU SAY IT, MEAN IT

Too many senior executives say things they don't really mean. What they often don't realize is that their subordinates and colleagues notice. As a result, they lose credibility. The last thing an executive wants to lose is credibility and the trust of the team.

A common one we all hear is, "My door is always open." The reality is that it's not always open. In fact, the door is shut half the time, and it takes weeks to get any face time. The statement is objectively false, both literally and figuratively.

If it isn't true, and you know it isn't true, don't say it. All you will do is degrade your own credibility and make your colleagues cringe or giggle behind your back every time they hear you throw out a commitment you won't keep—like, "My door is always open." If you say you're going to grant access to your team, then you'd better take concrete steps to make it happen. *Actions speak louder than words.*

By the way, your door doesn't have to be always open. Yes, being reachable and staying in regular contact is important, as we discussed in chapter 3. Employees don't expect an open-door policy of senior leaders. They know you're busy and can't drop everything the moment they walk in the door. A better way to think about this is in terms of *access.* I always give access to my team and stakeholders, even though my door may not be physically open.

I tell my teams that I like being transparent, sharing, collaborating, and being accessible through modern digital tools like WhatsApp, Slack, and, of course, SMS. My actions support what I say. I use WhatsApp regularly to keep my team informed and to build camaraderie. For example, if I'm at a senior leader meeting, I'll take pictures of what's going on—maybe of an impressive keynote presentation or a cool new restaurant—and I'll shoot it out to my team.

If you encourage this sort of digital communication by doing it yourself, even junior members of the team will feel like they're connected to you. They can send you an emoji, or a picture from a football game or from a restaurant you recommended to them.

If they're on a trip, they'll send me pictures and updates. I try to foster an environment where they feel comfortable sharing social pictures of them out at a bar or event.

CAUTION: CLEARING THE DECK CHAIRS

One of the things executives say when they land a new role or take over an existing team is, "Don't worry, I'm not going to make any big changes. You're all secure. It's business as usual." Then they'll meet with each team member, secretly sizing them up, determining their level of loyalty, and considering whether to get rid of them. One of the primary reasons this happens is the executive's desire for loyal soldiers.

Many inexperienced executives are hypersensitive to loyalty, especially when taking on a new role. They want to be absolutely certain that their team is loyal to them and will have their back. So, they "clear the deck chairs," which is a euphemism for firing a bunch of people. Then they fill those roles with their former colleagues whom they bring over from their previous company. I've seen this more times than I can count. Once the deck chairs are cleared and the old teammates and buddies are brought in, the executive thinks he can relax—he now has a loyal team.

Not so fast.

I actually see this quite differently. I've spent fifteen years in emerging markets where cultural norms are different than those in developed nations. In New York, if you lose a job, you send out resumes and you find another job. It doesn't work that way in emerging markets.

In Kenya, for example, many of the individuals working in any corporate environment are the first in their family ever to go to college. They're probably the principal breadwinner for the family. Because of this, and other cultural factors common in developing countries, when a family breadwinner gets fired it can be catastrophic.

The fired individual will probably be so ashamed that he won't even tell his wife. He's going to live with that secret until he, hopefully, finds another job. He'll likely even put on a suit and pretend he's still going to work every day.

The damage can be felt by the employer as well. When a corporation fires someone in a developing nation, there may be backlash. It can end up being a blemish on the company in that community, and the company's reputation and morale can take a hit.

Having seen these effects up close, I now have a different take on clearing the deck chairs. I advise against it. Especially if the goal is simply to build a loyal team, that's not the best way to go. Instead, I work with the team members to bring them into my camp and earn their loyalty through my actions—and I'm willing to put in the time to do it.

Don't think I'm an old softy or some kind of saint. Far from it. I never compromise on accountability and outcomes; business always needs to come first. Working with an existing team is better for the long-term good of an organization. It drives outcomes. It keeps morale higher. No one likes worrying about whether they'll be able to keep their job. No one wants to see their friends fired. In the age of social media, any disgruntled or ex-employee can do quite a bit of damage to a firm's reputation. Maintaining your team is better for employees, their families, and the community—especially in emerging markets.

Clearing the deck chairs can also have a negative impact on whatever industry you're in. It can reduce market share, and lost market share is difficult to regain. It also removes talented people from the workforce. The junior employees in a company will someday grow into leaders of the industry, provided they are given the proper support and guidance. How is someone going to learn and grow if you fire them instead of work with them and train them?

If they get fired through no fault of their own, but rather because they were hired by the previous leader, that hurts the company and the industry. A new leader may think it helps him when, in fact, it seriously damages his reputation. Clearing the deck chairs isn't about improving performance by hiring better people; it's about the leader eliminating his own insecurity.

Working with an existing team also makes the most financial sense. My philosophy is that developing people—training them, elevating them, promoting them from within, and giving them the tools to improve themselves—is where the greatest ROI lies. Executives who clear the deck chairs out of insecurity are misguided.

AMBASSADORS, SKEPTICS, AND DETRACTORS

As leaders and as human beings, we all want to feel like our people have our back. The truth is, not everyone on your team will support you at the beginning—some may never support you. Therefore, any executive coming in to take over an existing team needs to be able to identify the three types of team members, then learn how to deal with each.

The first group is made up of people I call the Ambassadors. These are the employees who sign up to your program right away. Your message, plan, and background resonate with them, so you won't have to put much effort into winning them over. They'll readily see you as the leader and get on board with your vision. Fantastic!

The second category of team members I call the Skeptics. They are sitting on the fence, and they're a little more skeptical of you and your intentions. They're taking a wait-and-see attitude toward you. Your instincts will tell you these people will take some work, but that you'll eventually be able to win them over. You have to be prepared to invest in those relationships and put in the time to build trust. You have to pay your dues by doing all the things we talked about in chapters 2 and 3. *Actions speak louder than words.*

The third category will be the most difficult to win over, if not impossible. This group is made up of people I call the Detractors—as in, *your* detractors. No matter what you do or how hard you work, this group will always be negative toward you. They are energy vampires and will cause you some sleepless nights. You need to identify these people as soon as possible. I advise you to always believe that they will come around, and that you will eventually win them over. Truth be told, you might—or you might not. Keep trying, but know that this will be the toughest group to deal with.

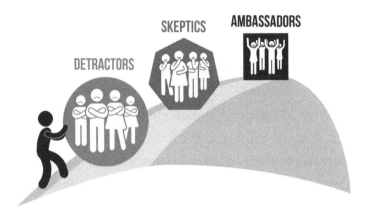

A good leader will treat employees in all three groups with equality and will invest in each. Don't show favoritism to people in the first group, because that will make converting the other groups even more difficult. It might even cause them to harden their stance toward you.

There may eventually come a time when you have to make a staff change. Keep trying to convert the Detractors until you reach a point of diminishing returns. For example, if their interactions become poisonous to the spirit of the team, to you personally, or to the organization, then you have to act. Ultimately, you may have to remove them from the team. Look at it through the lens of shareholder value: backstabbers who are poisoning the well won't permit anyone to do their best work, including you.

During this process, don't let your insecurities get out of check. Don't second-guess your employees or overanalyze them to figure out who supports you and who doesn't. Never ask, "Do you have my back? Because I have yours," even though you'll be thinking it. Obsessing over this will prevent you from putting points on the board and being *authentic*.

Instead, *Give to Get*; make sure your team knows that you always have their back, regardless of how they feel about you. That's the right path to stay on, no matter where their loyalties lie. As long as they believe you have their back, it doesn't matter whether they have yours.

There's no limit to the worlds you can conquer when your team feels safe and supported. The rewards and the wins will be massive.

SERVANT LEADERSHIP

The best way to get your team to have your back is to win their hearts and minds. As the title of this chapter suggests, words are not enough. It takes action—consistent action.

There is a management principle I love called *servant leadership*. It means the leader exists to serve those under him. In contrast, traditional leadership is a top-down pyramid where the leader sits at the top, and subordinates do as the leader commands. Servant leaders turn that pyramid upside down by sharing power with their teams, placing the needs of their team before their own, and helping subordinates develop and grow so they can perform at the highest level possible. Here are a few things that servant leaders do:

☑ COMMIT GENUINE ACTS OF EMPATHY AND SELF-SACRIFICE.

☑ TAKE BULLETS FOR THE TEAM SO THEY DON'T HAVE TO.

☑ STAND UP AND STAND TALL FOR THE TEAM WITH STAKEHOLDERS.

☑ PRIORITIZE TEAM LEARNING AND DEVELOPMENT AND FIND OPPORTUNITIES TO ACCELERATE SELF-DEVELOPMENT.

☑ CREATE AN EMPOWERING ATMOSPHERE AND ENCOURAGE THE TEAM TO TAKE RISKS BY LETTING THEM KNOW THEY'LL HAVE THE TEAM'S BACK IF THEY FAIL.

☑ ABOVE ALL, WALK THE TALK; SERVANT LEADERS MAKE SURE THEIR OWN ACTIONS ARE CONSISTENT WITH WHAT THEY EXPECT FROM THE TEAM.

SHOW ME THE SUN

If you've ever traveled to the Scandinavian countries in the wintertime, you know it's a cold and gloomy place because there is no sun for months on end. People get depressed and moody from the lack of sunshine. After a long, dark Scandinavian winter, you'll want to cry out, "Show me the sun!"

At the other extreme, during the summertime of the far northern latitudes the sun never sets. People have to go to bed with sunshine streaming in through the windows. That's enough to make you shout, "Too much sun!"

I developed my "show me the sun" theory while I was a partner at PricewaterhouseCoopers. At professional firms like PwC, the partners are often treated as demigods. All you have to do is watch an episode of the popular legal drama series *Suits*—the partners are like celebrities. For example, if a junior-level associate meets with a partner, it's considered a big deal. For junior staffers to have *any* contact with a partner is a big deal. All eyes follow partners as they stroll across an open floor. You get the idea.

In my "show me the sun" theory, any senior leader is the sun. Just like humans need to occasionally see sunshine to feel energized and alive, your clients need to see the sun once in a while. Without seeing any sun for long periods, the client relationship will start to malfunction. Deals will fall apart, stall, or implode.

As a senior leader, your presence and attention will energize the client, cast a warm glow on them, motivate them, and make them feel special. To keep your clients properly motivated, you must occasionally *show them the sun*.

But too much sun is not a good thing either.

The sun totally outshines everything else, including the moon and the planets. As an executive, you must be careful not to outshine your clients; and, more importantly, never outshine your team. You must make sure all the praise and credit goes to them, not to you. Your goal as a senior leader is to elevate your team, promote them, and make sure they get all the credit for a job well done.

The thing to remember about the "show me the sun" theory is balance. Too much sun and your team will be outshined, or your clients will start taking you for granted. Why would they ever call your director or senior manager when they can ring you, the senior leader, for the smallest of matters? Not enough sun and both your team and your clients, in particular, will feel neglected. It's imperative to find the right balance between sunshine and darkness.

So, show your clients *some* sun, and make sure you maintain that balance.

PUTTING THE TEAM FIRST

One of the best examples of a servant leader I've ever come across is my friend Lazarus. For a long time, he has been the CEO & president of GE Nigeria. This is a huge job that oversees GE's billions of dollars in assets and wide-ranging operations. GE sells aircraft engines, locomotives, electrical equipment, power generation, and medical equipment in Nigeria. Nigeria is the largest economy on the continent—even bigger than South Africa.

Lazarus is a geography leader for GE. That means he is not personally responsible for any one piece of business; rather, he oversees the entire territory. It's a complex role with many moving parts. He is a big *oga*—*oga* is a Yoruba word meaning "man in charge."

For Lazarus to be an effective geography leader, he's had to do all the things described in this book. He is legendary for his skills as a servant leader—famous for fighting hard for his people so they have the resources, money, and support they need to succeed. He fights for them ruthlessly and unapologetically, never backing down until he gets what his people need from headquarters. As a result, his teams always get more money, bigger budgets, more new hires, larger teams, more leverage, and whatever resources they need. I never saw anything like it.

Lazarus truly believed that he worked *for* his people. The only thing that mattered to him was *their* success. He knew that their success would in turn drive the success of the whole region.

Here's what that reputation did for him. It captured the hearts and minds of his people. His employees and clients loved him. When the quarterly results came in, so did the people in headquarters. His results were excellent year after year, all because he treated his job as a servant leader position.

THE BIG PICTURE

This story about Lazarus brings us back around to the title of this book, *Give to Get*. Lazarus is a great example of this philosophy in action. He gave his people so much, and in turn, he received even more.

By giving people the tools, resources, and support they need to perform at the highest level, senior leaders will receive in the form of better performance and more business in the books. By helping others, they also bring out the best in themselves. The path to fulfillment as a corporate leader doesn't run through the boardroom; it runs through others.

The race is long, and endurance is a must. A corporate career can span many decades. So, smart leaders use every big win and each success of their team as fuel to increase their fortitude, strength, and stamina.

CHAPTER 5

TAKING YOUR CREDIT TO THE BANK

Whether you're a senior leader or a junior executive, you must learn to demonstrate to your superiors that you're effective at your job. I'm not advocating grandstanding, seeking praise, or demanding adulation. Far from it. I am saying your career depends on your ability to make sure the company leaders know your value.

When I left PwC and joined GE, I went through all the steps and stages described earlier in this book. I navigated my way through the culture-within-a-culture, and I mapped my stakeholders and built a functional rhythm of communication with them. My team was finally up and running efficiently, and we were able to put points on the board. I woke up every morning thinking about how I could help my team succeed.

Then I noticed a problem.

After working so hard on many of the deals we closed, I was being sidelined. The recognition process seemed to skip past me. Yet I was quarterbacking the entire process. It really bothered me that I worked so hard cross-functionally to bring all the elements together to close a big piece of business, then got none of the credit.

Why was that?

Because the corporate world is not a warm and fuzzy place. People don't rush to wrap their arms around you when you score a big win. The opposite happens. After a huge deal closes, a complex war around who gets credit will inevitably break out. I recalled the premonition and wise counsel of Raghu Krishnamorthy, who was the vice president of executive development and chief learning officer for the company when I joined. As he understood my role, he needled me on my readiness to deal with this very issue.

He forewarned me that the salesperson who sold the deal would beat his chest like King Kong and try to take all the credit. Enablers and staffers with various functions will line up like a scene from the African savannah to drink out of the well of success. Years later, I remembered his forewarning when I saw carefully crafted emails flying back and forth with people effusively thanking one another for their contributions, and everyone scrambling to add their name to the list.

I thought putting deals together was complex; sorting out who gets credit is worse. I knew I had to figure out a system and a strategy that would ensure that I wasn't left out in the cold while everyone else was celebrating. I'm going to share that strategy with you later in this chapter.

LET YOUR TEAM SHINE

I have a good friend whose judgement and wisdom in this area I trust immensely. Andy was a senior human resources executive at GE who recently got promoted into a CEO role, and relocated to India to lead a business unit for GE. He's from a football family; his father coached a varsity team in the United States. So, he often explained corporate life through sports analogies.

Andy said senior leaders should create a game plan for getting credit long *before* points are scored. He said executives need to share their game plan for big deals with their superiors and stakeholders in advance. This is where the stakeholder mapping in chapter 3 comes into its own. As we discussed, you should be meeting regularly with your stakeholders, which includes your boss, to update them on what you're working on and what your priorities are. This is another way those regular touchpoints really benefit you.

When you share your game plan, your superiors and your stakeholders will know what your strategy is and how you want it to unfold. Then, every time your team reaches a milestone toward closing that deal, you can inform your stakeholders. These constant updates allow the stakeholders to follow along with the narrative in your playbook. They'll see it like a story being played out in front of them, and they'll buy in to your narrative.

By the time points are scored, it won't matter who tries to take credit for the win; the stakeholders will see you as the coach who created the strategy, executed it, and put the ball in the end zone. If you do this right and you're able to connect the outcomes to the narrative you shared with your stakeholders and updated them along the way, you'll certainly get credit for the win.

Andy added that senior executives *should* get credit for their work. As long as they're not grandstanding or bragging, it actually helps their superiors understand their effectiveness in that role. The core of being a leader is being effective. Don't feel that you're being self-serving in going after credit; if you do it properly, it's actually helpful to the company.

HOW TO CASH IN ON YOUR CREDIT

When it comes to taking credit for putting points on the board, there are relatively few people you need to convince. Those people are your superiors—your boss and your boss's boss, their peers, your mentors, and a few other powerful influencers high up in the company. I call those people "the bank" because they hold the power to compensate you in the form of bonuses and promotions for your hard work.

When you take your credit to the bank, be sure to show them your "bank statement." By this I mean showing the bankers your playbook and connecting the dots between your goals and objective, and the outcomes. As discussed in the previous section, this ensures that you get credit for putting those points on the board.

Taking your credit to the bank means all you have to do is make sure the most important people understand your involvement in the deal. There is no need to send out a mass email to the entire department, or to tell all the interns at the watercooler that you deserve all the credit. That's the equivalent of standing on a hill and shouting to anyone who will listen, "Look what I did!" All that does is make you feel good, and make your team feel like you're grabbing all the glory. It won't bring any form of short-term or long-term success to your bank account.

Let the spotlight-grabbing salesperson do that. He can run around the office telling everyone who will listen that he is the one who closed the deal. That's fine, let him. Meanwhile, you take your credit to the bank.

DON'T TELL THEM HOW HARD YOU WORKED FOR IT

The best gymnasts, swimmers, basketball players, or actors make greatness look easy. It's not easy, of course; winning championships or Oscars takes an incredible amount of work. To the audience it looks easy, so they assume that the athlete is just gifted, "a natural." That's the image you want to portray to the bank. You want them to think that closing big deals and making it rain comes naturally to you, that you're good at it because you have *talent*. Don't shatter that image by telling them how you had to grind it out in the trenches for months working fourteen-hour days. That kills the image. It also raises more questions than it answers: "Why was it so difficult? What did you do wrong?"

MAKE A SOCIAL CONTRACT WITH YOUR TEAM

It's not uncommon for a senior leader to have one or two team members go rogue and try to take all the credit for a big deal that closed, giving the senior leader no credit. Maybe they worked the hardest on the deal and feel entitled to the credit. Or perhaps their motivation is ambition or greed. Whatever the reason, this is something you want to prevent. It does not serve you. It may even make you look bad.

The best way to prevent this is to form a social contract with each of your team members. This is another example of *Give to Get*. You offer to give them something in return for what you want.

For example, a senior leader might say, "I really need this deal to close in this quarter. If you make that happen, I will support you in going for that promotion you want." That type of social contract creates a give-and-take relationship between the leader and the team member, aligning the stars naturally toward a successful outcome for both parties.

One of the results of this type of social contract is an interdependency between the two parties. Each person is relying on the other for something, and in turn must deliver something. This reduces the odds of either person backstabbing or slighting the other. They are both in this together with the same desired outcome: "I'm for you and you're for me."

This simple strategy can make sharing credit for big wins easier and more graceful. It can also help senior managers prevent getting backstabbed by their own people. Leaders who understand this concept are more well-mannered around the give-and-take of credit.

If you make a social contract with someone, it is absolutely imperative that you live up to your end of the agreement. If the other person delivers their side and you fail to deliver yours, that will undercut your credibility forever. Trust in you will be destroyed, with that person at the least, and perhaps with others as they will surely hear about it. *Actions speak louder than words.*

HELP YOUR SUPERIORS SHINE

You may be so focused on delivering outcomes and managing your team that you forget how important it is to make your superiors look good. Most senior leaders spend so much of their time shining the spotlight downward, they forget to look upward.

Your boss is a human being with an ego and a desire to

look good to his superiors too. He needs to get credit and accolades in front of *his* boss as well. In the right setting, perhaps a meeting of senior leaders, I would often say things like, "Phil had the vision on this deal. We just executed his vision." Or, "It's been an unbelievable year. With Phil's leadership, look what we've accomplished."

Complimenting your boss in a sincere and deserving way in front of his superiors, peers, and influencers will go a long way. Very often, executives forget to do that. They always hustle to make their team look good, but it never occurs to them to make their boss look good.

STEPPING INTO A GREAT LEADER'S SHOES

One of the most challenging situations an executive can get into is replacing a great leader. By great leader, I mean someone who delivered impressive results, built up an entire division or company, was adored by everyone, was respected by the community, and was all-around very successful in his role. Replacing someone like that is tough because, in all likelihood, the replacement won't be as good as the original. The best way to win in this situation is to excel in a totally different way.

My friend Bob Collymore found himself in this exact situation. He took over as CEO of a company called Safaricom in Kenya. Safaricom is an enormously successful telecom company, run for years by a beloved CEO named Michael Joseph. Michael was a legendary CEO who was revered by his employees and the shareholders.

When Bob took over as CEO after Michael retired, he knew what he was up against. There was no way he could fill Michael's shoes. Bob decided he would not try to be like Michael at all; instead, Bob pivoted. He adopted a leadership style that was strong in the areas where Michael was weak. Bob was more accessible, less aloof. He was more of a people's leader, less of an aristocrat. Bob invested more in local talent and mentoring. Most importantly, Bob never disparaged or criticized Michael.

The magic worked. In a short span, the employees and shareholders of Safaricom realized Bob Collymore was an excellent CEO, just in a different way than Michael Joseph had been. Bob played it right; he took the role and made it his own. If he had tried to be a carbon copy of Michael, he would likely have failed. Today, Safaricom is synonymous with Bob Collymore; he is the face, the ambassador, and the bedrock of the company.

THE LONG ROAD TO SUCCESS

If you're reading this book, you're already a corporate

leader, or on your way to becoming one. You need to accept that the road to career success is long. It takes decades. As we've discussed throughout this book, it requires fortitude, patience, foresight, and endurance.

There will be many glorious moments, many trophies and big wins, and many good days. There will also be many hard days and many demoralizing defeats. Jack Ma, the billionaire Chinese founder of Alibaba, recently admitted that he's had more dark days than good days. I was in the audience when he said it, and we were all stunned. This was one of the richest men on the planet, and there he was saying he's had more bad days than good.

I believe failures are necessary. When leaders in big corporations are recruiting candidates, they look to those failures to see that you had them, how you pivoted from them, and what you learned from them. Were you able to endure and bounce back?

People who've succeeded despite past failures are the kind of people I want on my team. They have the resilience to get back up and the endurance to keep going. I'll share some of my failures in the next chapter.

NO PLACE TO GO BUT UP

When I was a partner at PricewaterhouseCoopers, I had many great wins: a first-of-its-kind public offering for a state-owned power generation company, a record-setting acquisition, a historic public-private enterprise, iconic infrastructure builds, and plenty of prestigious awards, including international awards and various pan-Africa awards.

However, I suffered many setbacks and failures as well—missed numbers, deals lost to competitors, market poaches, privatizations gone bad, lost investments, team issues, and so on. That comes with the job, and I accept it as a part of doing business. One loss in particular I feel deep scars from even today.

A staffer of mine was a non-equity director at PwC. He wanted to be partner. I had worked with him for many years, and watched him grow and move up the ranks. He was a tremendous ambassador for the company, a complete loyalist to the firm, a great role model to the team, reliable, talented, hard-working, and he always delivered outcomes. In my estimation, he'd proved that he deserved to make partner.

I put my own reputation on the line for him when I formally backed him for partnership. He deserved it, and I was happy to endorse him. I lobbied the other partners hard on his behalf. In the end, the promotion never came, and we lost him to Ernst and Young. He left PwC as a director, and he joined Ernst and Young as an equity partner.

I was crushed.

In my view, PwC had let a valuable asset go to the competition. My feelings of failure were intense—I lost a member of my team whom I'd not been able to help elevate to partnership. Elevating members of my team and helping them succeed is something I pride myself on; and this time, I failed. It was a big loss for me on many levels. Despite my having personally put my name and reputation behind his bid for partnership, in the end, I was not able to convince the other partners. That hurt. My career has been built on elevating, promoting, and mentoring talented people. This failure on my part was a bitter disappointment.

In any executive's career, there will be a series of both wins and losses. The key to longevity is to figure out a strategy for accepting and dealing with those losses *quickly* so you can move rapidly to the next milestone.

OVERCOMING FEAR OF FAILURE

I have seen corporate executives become crippled by fear of failure. When they face a big obstacle or a tenacious competitor, all they can think about is, "What if I lose? Will I still have a job?" They become so worried about losing that they can't focus on what they should be doing—executing. In a sense, they end up defeating themselves.

Over the course of my career, I've had those same thoughts and worries. When your entire year comes down to one huge deal or project, it's human nature to worry. But you must dismiss those thoughts and execute your plan. Some of the most successful companies and individuals are worth billions because they took risks and executed. Without risk there is no reward.

In times like this, I think of fearful images of curtains of smoke caused by a crash in a Formula One car race. The smoke is so thick that the other drivers can't see what's beyond it. That's terrifying when you're driving 180 miles per hour. The drivers who win are the ones who trust that everything will be fine on the other side of that smoke— they step on the gas, not the brake. Yes, it's a risk, but with that risk comes tremendous reward.

Drive fearlessly through the curtain of smoke on life's racetrack, and victory awaits you!

That sums up my philosophy when it comes to fear in the corporate setting. Step on the gas! Go bigger and bolder. Embrace the risk involved. That's the way to win. If you take your foot off the accelerator and coast when things get scary, you'll never win.

It may not seem like it at the time, but failure is not always a terrible thing. Failure helps develop *grit*. I believe my failures have given me fortitude and courage to go forward. Having experienced failure, I know what it feels like, and I know I can bounce back and get through it. I see all failures as nothing more than temporary setbacks, speedbumps on the road to success.

Fear of failure often limits an executive's ability to act decisively and take action. Getting over that fear of failing and instead embracing risk is the antidote to inaction. Some corporate cultures actually embrace failure for this very reason; it allows teams to place big bets and make moves without the fear of failure. As a result, these companies tend to be fast and nimble.

FAIL FAST

I've heard people in the start-up community say, "The best thing is to succeed, but the second-best thing is to fail fast." I agree with that, and I strongly believe it applies to the corporate world, not just to start-ups.

Unfortunately, when corporate leaders commit to investing in a project, they tend to stick with it long after it's obvious to everyone that it's going to fail. "Let's just stay the course through year end and then reassess." This is largely because no one wants to admit they made the wrong decision, so they stick with it hoping things will turn around.

The irony is that admitting the mistake and correcting course quickly is often the best answer. It prevents more money from being wasted; allows the team to consider new solutions, pivot, and recalibrate; and frees up resources and staff for deployment in other parts of the company. I'm a big believer in cutting my losses if it looks like the ROI is never going to be there.

A quick and merciful end to a failing program is more humane than letting it limp on endlessly for years, draining resources, and causing undue stress. Someone once said to me, "I would rather commit career suicide than suicide by career." I totally agree. By admitting my project was a misfire, I might eventually find myself out of a job. But that would be preferred to managing a failing program that causes extreme stress, team infighting, and endless sleepless nights caused by trying to right a sinking ship.

You are the first person who will know when something isn't going to work. Your gut instinct will tell you. If you stick with a project after you know it's going to fail, you're lying to yourself. You're lying to your team and to your boss. You're lying to your shareholders and stakeholders. Come clean, admit the truth, and pivot to something that works.

TIMING IS EVERYTHING

I believe in decisive decision making and taking action with immediacy and intensity. Speed is critical in the corporate world. Those who are fast win; the slow get left behind. But that does *not* mean you can be reckless. There is no excuse for making a rash and ill-considered decision. You can be careful and deliberate about decision making and still work with intensity and urgency.

When making big, important decisions, such as when to bring the ax down on a failing program or making a staff change, pay close attention to the timing. If you announce an important decision at the wrong time, it could affect the outcome in a negative way. If you announce it at the optimal time, there is a higher likelihood of success.

When is the *optimal* time to announce a change, especially a big change? The answer is right after you've had a big win and have put points on the board. Let's say you have a project that is failing and you want to announce that you're shutting it down. Wait until you have a big deal closed, put points on the board, and then, while you're still surrounded by the glow of that deal, make the announcement. This is being strategic about timing.

When you're basking in the glow of a big win, have a list of all the changes you want to make. Perhaps it's a personnel change on your team, or a personal change for yourself. Create a priority list, and then, when those big successes happen, you can trade in some of those points.

Beware that too much rapid change at once will alienate people. It's important to understand that part of human nature. I've seen something as innocuous as a project or department name change wind people up. It caught me off guard at first. But then I realized there were employees who had worked at the company under the same name for decades. They had no idea a name change was under consideration, so they were blindsided. In certain cases, it's better to make decisions slowly by applying gentle pressure, rather than all of a sudden.

Understand that this concept of timing in the corporate world will take some practice. Think of it as learning to drive a car. When you first learned to drive, it was difficult to judge the timing. But, with experience, you began to understand when to step on the gas and how hard, when to brake and how hard, and when to stop. Eventually, the timing part of driving became second nature to you.

CREATE YOUR PLAYBOOK

Just like every new business needs a business plan, the senior leader needs a written plan detailing how they're going to meet their objectives for the year, broken down by quarter. I call it a playbook. The playbook lists every key piece of business that an executive intends to close, and then lays out the detailed steps and strategy to make it happen.

Think of a playbook for a football team. The coach will rewrite the playbook a dozen times during a football season as things change. In fact, coaches will often change the playbook *within* a single game, usually at halftime. A key player might get hurt, or new opponents and new information becomes available, necessitating a change in strategy. The coach studies the playbook constantly, always has it with him, and updates it as needed.

Similarly, your playbook is your game plan. It can and should change throughout the year as new obstacles arise and new information becomes available. Think of it as a living, evolving roadmap to success. I probably change my playbook three to five times each year. Some are major changes to strategy. Others are just course-correcting when the unexpected happens. The end goals and objectives do not change, only the route to get there does.

A detailed playbook is something that will help every executive stay on track, on schedule, and on target for reaching their goals. Changes to the playbook can help keep things interesting and keep your team engaged. The playbook will instill in the leader a greater passion, responsibility, and sense of purpose. But most of all, it will lay out the roadmap to having a great year. All you have to do is refer to it often and follow it.

"LET'S TRY THIS AGAIN."

There is no set format for a playbook. Each one will vary by industry, role, department, region, and so on. But all playbooks have certain core elements. First, include exactly *why* you want to achieve the objectives in this playbook. Be as personal as you can. Second, include the overall goals of your division or department within the company. Next, include a list of the key team members you need to rely on to achieve these objectives. Then, include a detailed description of exactly what you're going to accomplish and how you're going to accomplish it. Finally, include detailed numbers and metrics along with every specific goal you plan to achieve.

CHAPTER 7

OVERCOMING UNDERWHELM

I was recently talking to a very senior executive working for a major multinational corporation who said he was feeling "underwhelmed" in his job. The job he had a few years earlier was as a commercial leader and market-facing CEO for a smaller, but still substantial business. He left that company for what he believed would be a bigger opportunity.

When I asked him why he was feeling underwhelmed, he said he didn't feel challenged or utilized up to the level of his experience and capabilities. It wasn't about his title or his compensation; he said those were in line with his expectations. What he had a problem with was his role, his leverage within the company, and the lack of intellectual challenge. He said, "They're underutilizing me. I am capable of so much more. I can deliver mountains. But they have me shoveling small piles."

UNDERWHELM CAN BE OVERWHELMING

That specific flavor of dissatisfaction is incredibly common in the senior ranks at big corporations. I've heard that same sentiment hundreds of times during my career as a senior leader. I learned to spot it a mile away. A senior leader would be hired in from the outside, and during their first year or two they would begin to experience withdrawal symptoms. They missed the feeling of moving mountains at their previous firm. Now they felt underutilized and underwhelmed. Some thought they were hired to do certain very high-level tasks, but the work that actually fell on them was much less important.

The way most successful executives I've known have tried to fight that underwhelm was by really digging into their role. They would summon a great burst of energy, bring an impressive amount of commercial intensity to their work, and get fully engrossed in it. As a result, they would deliver tasks assigned to them quickly. But as soon as the high of accomplishment wore off, they'd be back to feeling underwhelmed.

The worst way to react to corporate underwhelm is to let it affect your work and your attitude in the office. Getting depressed, moping around the halls, showing up late, losing your drive—these are things that can kill your reputation. Don't fall into that trap.

You cannot beat yourself down too much. If you let yourself feel depressed and sad in the office, it will start to show on your face and in your body language. Others will notice. Your team will notice. They will see this as a weakness exposed. It won't be inspiring to your team or your stakeholders, and they may begin to question your effectiveness.

Left unchecked, underwhelm often ends with the executive applying for a transfer or leaving the company entirely. I've heard more than a few colleagues say, "This isn't worth it. I don't want to wake up in the morning and do this anymore. I'm not having fun."

I believe corporates should form support groups or mentorship programs for their senior teams to share, collaborate, and learn from one another's experiences. At the time of this writing, there is a popular television series on Showtime titled *Billions*. It's about a group of high achievers who run a hedge fund in New York. In the show, lead character Bobby Axelrod understands the need to constantly reprogram his high performers, so he has a full-time, in-house shrink on staff to keep them functioning at the highest level. I am not suggesting corporates rush to hire a full-time therapist, but I am suggesting that senior staff in particular need someone to chat with and learn from in a safe, collaborative environment.

WHY UNDERWHELM HAPPENS

What I learned in chatting with many mentees, peers, and senior executives over my career is that this underwhelm syndrome tends to affect intense, hard-charging, type A personalities the most. I think it's because they get so keyed up and laser-focused when they're in the middle of a big deal. When it's over their adrenalin and energy crash hard, leaving them at a low point and missing the high. The more even-keeled personalities who can go with the flow more easily don't seem to be as susceptible to underwhelm.

There's also a corporate structure reason for underwhelm. Everyone knows that big companies like GE, Amazon, Microsoft, Google, P&G, AT&T, Facebook, the Wall Street banks, and the consultancies have the ability and the resources to recruit the best and brightest talent in business. If you're at the top of your class at Harvard Business School, these companies will fight over you. Recruiting is not their problem.

Their problem is keeping all those bright minds engaged in a way that's fulfilling to them. It's a sad truth that while big corporations are great at recruiting, they actually suck at utilizing top talent to the best of their abilities. Once they hire a top recruit, big corporations are horrible at embracing them, leveraging their skills, capitalizing on their strengths, keeping them happy, and building ideal, sustainable roles for them.

This is one of the single largest root causes of underwhelm. It's why there's a lot of mobility between companies at the more senior executive levels. Many top executives have taken an almost mercenary-like attitude toward their career where they'll jump to the highest bidder, from one company to the next.

PAUSE AND STEP BACK

If you find yourself suffering from corporate underwhelm, there is a strategy to combat it. That strategy is rooted in something my father used to say to me. "In any bad situation," he would say, "you can only change yourself. You can't count on changing the situation or the people around you." In other words, each of us holds the power to overcome any obstacle by looking inward, not outward.

If you are experiencing underwhelm, the first thing to do

is pause and step back. Do not make rash decisions, such as blaming the employer. I've heard too many executives say things like, "It's the company's fault this isn't working out. They're to blame for my skills being underutilized. They never should have hired me."

Another rash decision that's quite common is quitting or looking for another job. What happens if you go through all that trouble to get a different job and within a few months you're back to feeling underwhelmed again?

After you pause and step back, go back and review your playbook. Did you set goals for yourself that are too low? Maybe that's why you don't feel challenged. Can you increase your goals to make them more difficult to reach? Up your aspirations?

Study your playbook and look for hidden opportunities you may have missed. Is there an opportunity for a pivot? Can you recalibrate the playbook and get creative about reaching new or existing goals? That's what leaders do; they constantly reassess and look for new ways forward. Consider new strategies. Brainstorm innovations. Just the exercise of reexamining your playbook with some of these steps will start to lift the underwhelm.

Remember that you were hired because of your talents

and abilities. Just because you're feeling underwhelmed doesn't change that. Always carry yourself with regality and confidence—like the lion, no matter how much you may feel like a goat. Your team looks up to you, so always act and behave like someone who deserves their admiration and respect. *You have to act like a king if you want to be treated like one.*

TRY JOB CRAFTING

There's another useful strategy that I recommend for overcoming underwhelm in almost any job. You may have heard of it; it's called "job crafting."

In 2001, two university professors began studying how workers in boring or tedious jobs coped with the grind of their daily work routine. Jane Dutton from the University of Michigan and Amy Wrzesniewski from Yale University found that workers who were able to expand their job description and contribute to a greater goal were happier and more effective on the job.

In their research, Dutton and Wrzesniewski found that hospital janitors who focused on their larger contribution to healing and to the healthcare system fared better and suffered less burnout. They created the term "job crafting."

According to an article titled "'Job Crafting': The Great Opportunity in the Job You Already Have," published on Forbes.com, "Job crafting means essentially this: That people often take existing job expectations—or job descriptions—and expand them to suit their desire to make a difference. In other words, job crafters are those who do what's expected (because it's required) and then find a way to add something new to their work—something that benefits their team, their company, or their customer."

Job crafting can be a powerful tool to help executives avoid burnout and find new meaning in their work. The best part about it is that job crafting is virtually unlimited. There are endless ways to expand and grow almost any job description. So, look into job crafting; there's a lot of information out there about how it works and the powerful benefits it provides.

FIND YOUR OWN SOLUTION

Being happy in a job is much like being happy in a marriage. You first have to realize that you can't change your spouse. You can only change yourself. There's no use complaining that your spouse doesn't live up to your expectations in some way. Rather, you should focus on how *you* can transform *yourself* into the kind of partner that your spouse will admire and respond to.

Take a moment to reflect on your own strengths, weaknesses, and talents. Think about what changes you can make in *yourself* to excel at your current job. Don't try to figure out how to change the job to fit you. Figure out what you need to do in order to reach your full potential within the context of your current situation.

If the job is not challenging you, figure out how you can challenge yourself. Can you raise your revenue or profit goals for the year? Can you pursue new deals that may not even be in your playbook? Can you help out on other interesting projects cross-functionally within the company? Think about ways to challenge yourself that will allow you to reach your full potential.

When I reflect back on my career, it is crystal clear to me that what I enjoyed most was problem solving for clients and customers, and mentoring young executives to help them grow and advance. Fighting for revenue, transactional activity, operational excellence, or economic gain was never the be-all and end-all for me. I did all that, of course, but it didn't give me a high as much as problem solving and lifting others up.

What really makes me come alive is seeing my mentees getting promoted, building their skills, growing with the organization, and utilizing some of the strategies I taught them to become successful. That's the part of the job I love. That was always my ROI. When I'm doing that, I experience no underwhelm. I actively looked for more and more opportunities to mentor people at work. Eventually, my underwhelm disappeared.

In order to transform yourself, you have to know yourself first. You need clarity about who you are and what energizes you. The answer is different for everyone. For me, it was mentoring young people and helping them succeed, or working with clients to find answers to complex problems. For you, it could be personal financial success or closing deals. When you figure out what makes you happy on the job, you'll be more likely to pursue it with greater passion, which will in turn prevent you from being underwhelmed.

Bottom line: if you are experiencing underwhelm, you have the power to make a positive change. There is no point in sitting on the HR person's couch, saying, "I'm feeling underwhelmed." HR can't fix it for you. Your boss can't fix it. If you're at a multinational like GE, even the chairman can't fix it for you. The only person who can fix it is you.

CHAPTER 8

OVERCOMING BURNOUT

Over the last decade of my corporate career, I became an active angel investor in a number of business ventures outside of my corporate job. I made tech investments and angel investments in local and regional start-ups in Africa. I put together a partnership to buy the high-rise office tower in which PricewaterhouseCoopers has its offices. I helped my wife and her sister open one of the most popular award-winning restaurants in Nairobi, called Urban Eatery. I also cofounded a successful invitation-only business club, Capital Club, which is now part of a family of three other international locations, and growing.

The benefit of that outside investment activity was that it provided me a window into entrepreneurial and small business activity outside of my corporate bubble. It gave me a good sense of what was happening with the business community at ground level in various African markets. While in my corporate job, I often felt like I was flying at 40,000 feet above sea level, and just working on billion-dollar mega-projects.

Angel investing also provided me a terrific opportunity to interact with African entrepreneurs and businesses. These entrepreneurs weren't necessarily alums of Harvard, Wharton, or McKinsey. I could feel the local winds in each of the areas where I had investments. I got to know the local talent pool and labor markets. This gave me keen insights that I was able to apply in my corporate role. It made me more multidimensional, and more valuable as an executive.

What I like most about my angel investments is that they helped me overcome a very real risk for senior leaders: burnout.

GET CLEAR ON YOUR *WHY*

After a long, successful career with PricewaterhouseCoopers, I chose to leave and join GE. It was a senior career move that raised a lot of eyebrows. "Vishal is a partner; why on earth is he leaving?" The reason I left has to do with finding my *why*.

You may be familiar with popular author Simon Sinek, who wrote the groundbreaking books *Start with Why* and *Find Your Why*. Sinek argues that everyone should look deep inside themselves to find out *why* they truly want the things they want. That *why*, he says, will be the guiding force for achievement.

I loved PwC, and I had many good years there. I left PwC to join GE because, at that point in my career, my *why* aligned well with what GE was trying to achieve in Africa. I had worked with GE for years from the outside; they were a PwC client. I saw firsthand what they were doing and how they were doing it.

GE was trying to open up new markets and bring exciting new infrastructure solutions to Africa. As a resident of Kenya and a frequent traveler all over the continent, I knew how badly Africa needed that infrastructure. It was essential to our growth. GE had the *why* that deeply resonated with me.

As an angel investor, I looked at many deals that needed reliable infrastructure to succeed. Plus, infrastructure projects really can have an immediate and profound positive effect on broader communities. The opportunity to make a positive impact for the region was incredibly attractive to me. It was a very powerful *why*, and I jumped on it.

If GE's pitch to get me on board was, "Hey, Vishal, we want you to help us sell gas turbines so we can all make big bonuses," I would have said no. I had no interest in just selling a product to make more money. I wanted something that aligned with my values and my *why*. Now, how I approach all my businesses, build my teams, assess markets, launch products, and even how I run my personal life all start with my *why*.

Knowing your *why* is one of the surest ways to avoid burnout.

BURNOUT

I was always confused when I would see accomplished executives with fifteen or twenty years of experience, usually at the top of their game, quit the company and do something completely different. Or, sometimes, they'd transfer to a different division of the company where they had no experience. For example, at PwC a partner in audit would unexpectedly announce one day that he's moving to the tax department. When asked, they would usually say something like, "I just needed a change."

Why would senior executives in their forties or fifties at the peak of their careers decide to go and do something else? One word: burnout.

Burnout is incredibly common in the corporate world, especially among senior leaders. There are many factors that cause burnout. It starts with the heavy burden of responsibility that senior leaders have. They must deliver results. They have specific revenue goals hanging over their head all year long. That playbook stares up at them from their desk every day, and they know they'll be measured by how they perform. All the while, formidable competitors are competing relentlessly against them for the same business.

Meanwhile, the executive's family is demanding more of his time and attention. The executive has missed too many school plays, dance recitals, soccer games, and parent-teacher conferences. He begins to see the same old disappointment register on his family's faces. A sadness sets in after having missed out on so much of the children's lives.

Add to all this the stress of recruiting, hiring, firing, motivating, and managing a team of highly intelligent individuals. Each one of them has their own needs, desires, and problems. Team members often suffer burnout as well.

By necessity, most executives operate at a very high performance level sixty or more hours per week. The stress is tremendous. The anxiety is through the roof. The travel is exhausting. The phone and email never shut off. Being a corporate leader takes its toll.

So, it's not surprising that many senior leaders wake up one day and wonder, *Why am I doing this?* They find themselves in a sort of existential career crisis. They realize they're just going through the motions. They feel like they're suffocating and start looking for a way out. They begin plotting their escape from the golden handcuffs of corporate life.

Almost no one at the senior level of a major corporation is immune to burnout after so many years in the trenches. Luckily, there's a solution. It starts with recognizing that you might have a *why* problem.

YOU MIGHT HAVE A *WHY* PROBLEM

Columnist David Brooks penned a wonderful piece in the *New York Times* in 2015 titled "The Moral Bucket List." Brooks writes, "It occurred to me that there were two sets of virtues, the résumé virtues and the eulogy virtues. The résumé virtues are the skills you bring to the marketplace. The eulogy virtues are the ones that are talked about at your funeral." That struck me as an apt way to divide any executive's career into two parts.

The first fifteen years or so of a corporate career are

devoted to building up your list of skills and experience. In other words, executives often focus on building up their resumes. These "resume virtues" grow to include an important title, a large corner office, a high salary and big bonuses, and more responsibility.

After fifteen or more years of building up the resume, your resume is full. At this point, most corporate executives want more. They're no longer happy with just a fancy title, perks, and a lucrative compensation package. They want to make a difference. They want to have an impact on the company, the industry, and the world around them. These are what Brooks calls the "eulogy values"—what people are going to remember you for at your funeral.

My eulogy values have been expressed pretty clearly in the preceding pages. At my funeral, I want to be recognized as someone who lifted people up, mentored young leaders, helped them become their best self, opened up markets, built iconic infrastructure projects, and contributed greatly to Africa. Those are my values and my *why* for getting up and going to the office every day.

ESCAPE BY GOING DEEPER

If you're experiencing the symptoms of burnout, your emotions will be telling you to just leave. But quitting a job may not solve your problems. In fact, quitting often creates even more stress than staying in a difficult job. Now you're anxious because you're unemployed and have no income. You're also worried that you may have seriously hurt your career by leaving a great job. Quitting is seldom the right move.

The better course of action involves going deeper. Delve deeper into your *why*. Delve deeper into your eulogy virtues. Figure out what it is that makes your hair stand up. What makes you spring out of bed in the morning? What puts a smile on your face? What are your unique gifts and strengths? What are you naturally talented at doing? And perhaps my favorite question: What makes you tick?

It's essential that you figure out your *why* and your eulogy virtues. Why are you doing what you're doing? Why are you working so hard? Why are you so dedicated to this job that keeps you away from your family two weeks each month? Does your *why* align with your values and your aptitude?

If you're having trouble answering these questions, then you have a *why* problem. If you don't know why you're doing such an intense corporate job, then you're probably headed for trouble. Uncovering your *why* is a huge leap toward avoiding burnout.

REFLECTION

I came to understand my own *why*, and my eulogy virtues, only after considerable introspection, reflection, and self-assessment. This may take some time, but the end result is worth it. Knowing why you're doing this job will become your internal compass. It will guide you through good days and dark days, over calm seas and rough seas. It will fuel your endurance. More importantly, it will help you pursue action and move forward toward the right path for you.

My path focused on coaching and mentoring the next generation of emerging corporate leaders and entrepreneurs, as well as angel investing. It has brought me much happiness and fulfillment. It also gives me confidence, meaning, and purpose. It makes me jump out of bed in the morning. Helping others succeed is perfectly aligned with my eulogy virtues and my *why*. Perhaps sharing your knowledge and mentoring young people may also be a path that appeals to you.

But since everyone is different, there is no one right path. You'll have to find your own way based on your own *why* and how you want to be remembered. While the paths may be different for all of us, the happiness and fulfillment that are waiting for you on the other side are universal.

CONCLUSION

COMING FULL CIRCLE

Over the past two and a half decades, I've had the honor and privilege of working for two of the most innovative, forward-thinking, and iconic corporations on the planet. I spent some of the best years of my life at PricewaterhouseCoopers. GE will always be the *Great* Electric company to me. I have many good friends at each, and I miss them dearly.

It truly has been an incredible journey. The fast-paced, often hectic lifestyle of a senior leader at a multinational corporation affords many benefits, and even more challenges. My corporate career has provided me not just with financial gain, but also intellectual riches beyond anything I had imagined early in my career.

INVESTING IN AFRICA

I am an active investor in Africa's future. My private investment firm, Full Circle Africa, is charging full steam ahead. We fund and manage a portfolio of early-stage investments; fund industrial equipment, which is essential and outrageously slow to finance; and play local-development partner to a select group of clients—entirely in Africa.

Thanks again for reading my book. I hope you found it to be worthwhile and a good investment of your time.

I wish you many years ahead of always being a lion. Never a goat.

VISHAL AGARWAL

FULLCIRCLE.AFRICA | GIVETOGETBOOK.COM

FOLLOW ME ON:

TWITTER: VISHALSVOICE

LINKEDIN: VISHALAGARWALAFRICA

ABOUT THE AUTHOR

VISHAL AGARWAL has lived the corporate lifecycle from start to finish, beginning as an intern and working up to senior deals partner at PricewaterhouseCoopers. Until recently, Vishal was a Global Top 500 Senior Leader for General Electric before becoming chairman & CEO of his own private investment management firm, Full

Circle Africa. During his twenty-four-year career, he has navigated all facets of corporate life from building teams and delivering value to translating multinational visions into local wins.

A true globalist, Vishal was born in Bombay, lived in Iran during the Iran–Iraq War, was educated through his adolescence in the United States, and now lives in Nairobi, Kenya, with his wife and two daughters.